CW00519652

Conceptual Understanding in Mathematics: A Handbook on the Reasoning Behind Selected Mathematical Topics

by Brian R. Evans

Pace University, New York

Table of Contents

Introduction

This brief handbook is intended for educators, parents/guardians, students, or anyone simply interested in understanding the reasoning behind selected basic, and not so basic, mathematical topics. Another intention of the handbook is to present the reader with a selected group of counterintuitive results found in mathematics, which would prove interesting for the reader and for students in mathematics.

Despite the emphasis on understanding in the educational research literature and teacher education programs, many students continue to learn mathematics procedurally with a lack of real conceptual understanding. Research shows that many new teachers revert to teaching the way they were taught when they were in school, and not the way they were taught to teach in their teacher education programs. Moreover, teachers often claim that they believe in teaching for understanding and through problem solving, but continue to teach their students procedural knowledge only. Perhaps for some teachers it can be a lack of understanding in their own mathematical background that prevents them from teaching from an understanding perspective.

When a person learns mathematics procedurally without real understanding, he or she is more likely to later forget what was learned rather than if the mathematics if fully understood initially. This handbook is intended for those interested in knowing the "why" behind selected mathematical concepts. Further, this book presents mathematics in a motivating way to make the subject more interesting. There is a reciprocal relationship between understanding and enjoying mathematics because people generally find mathematics more interesting when they truly understand what they are learning.

The reader may feel that he or she already knows much of the mathematics presented in this handbook. Admittedly, much of the mathematics is quite basic. However, I would guess that for many readers the conceptual understanding behind the concepts will be new. Therefore, even if the reader can perform operations, it is beneficial to understand the reasoning behind the methods, which is the aspect of this book that will be valuable for many readers. While procedures can be forgotten, it is much less likely that understanding will be will be lost and this will enable the reader to "figure out" how to perform operations contained in this handbook, as well as possibly unfamiliar operations not covered in this book.

The tragedy is that those who lack solid mathematical understanding and skills are at quite a disadvantage in life. It has been said that one of the most important skills a job applicant can have is strong mathematical knowledge. H. G. Well once said, "Statistical thinking will one day be as necessary for efficient citizenship as the ability to read and write." Perhaps we can say the same of mathematical thinking in general. Instead of "one day," perhaps we can say "now." Researcher and mathematics education professor Rochelle Gutierrez has called mathematics a "gatekeeper," which means that mathematics is perhaps a necessary, but not sufficient, condition for future success in college and career, and knowledge and proficiency in mathematics is needed for upward mobility. It seems that at least once a year, if not more often, I read a news article finding that most of the highest paying jobs have one thing in common: mathematics.

In mathematics education, researchers and educators try to find how to best gain mathematical understanding for all students. Sadly, many mathematics classrooms in the United States focus too heavily on procedural knowledge and do not spend enough time on conceptual knowledge. It is when students conceptualize the mathematical content that they gain an understanding and are less likely to forget what they have learned, and with conceptual understanding students will be better equipped to handle procedural mathematics. Yes, conceptual understanding is initially more time consuming and takes great effort from both the teacher and student. However, the gains will far outweigh the time and effort involved.

In the Trends in International Mathematics and Science Study (TIMSS) and Program for International Student Assessment (PISA) it was found that of developed nations the United States generally ranks lower in mathematics and science as other countries such as Singapore, South Korea, Japan, and Finland. Recently the United States has improved its ranking since the first iteration of the TIMSS study appeared in 1995, possibly due to the increased effort to improve mathematics and science education in this country. When observing how teachers teach in high achieving nations, there are stark differences. In high achieving East Asian countries the focus in mathematics is on covering select topics more deeply. In the United States there is too much emphasis on

10

covering as much material as possible rather than fully developing a smaller select set of topics. Students in the United States too often learn very little about a topic before moving to the next topic. Usually what is learned is typically forgotten by the end of the academic year, most certainly by the next academic year, and in many cases forgotten even before a major test.

So what can be done to alleviate the mathematics education crisis in the United States? The answer to this question is open to much debate. I believe it would be helpful to reduce the topics learned in the classroom, which is no easy task to do. How will we decide what is important and what can be taken out of the curriculum? This is a difficult task, certainly, but not an impossible one. Moreover, how can we be certain that our students are learning mathematics from a conceptual perspective? My favorite word in a mathematics class is "why." I often ask my students why they got the answer they did. When they tell me how they found their answers, I further probe as to why this algorithm, or method for solving, works the way it does. This method of teaching is how we can best help students to learn mathematics for true understanding.

Probably the three most commonly used words when discussing classroom management for new teachers are trust, consistency and engagement. Creating a caring classroom environment in which students feel the teacher has their best interest is critical for effective management. Second, if we tell students there will be a consequence for a certain action or a result from particular efforts, we should be fully prepared to follow through with that action. If we do not, our words will not be trusted in the future. The final major focus is engagement. How can we best engage our students? If we are able to engage our students in the lessons, they will be less likely to cause classroom disruptions and more likely to learn and succeed. Unfortunately, many students, and adults as well, find the study of mathematics incredible dry and boring. And rightfully so! As taught in many classrooms, mathematics can be awfully boring. I cannot help but think about John Paulos' concern in *Innumeracy: Mathematical Illiteracy and Its Consequences*, in which Paulos chides those who flaunt their mathematical illiteracy with comments such as, "I always hated math" and "I've always been terrible in mathematics." It should come as no surprise that many hold a strong dislike for mathematics considering the way they have learned the subject. If we want students to be engaged and learn well, then we need to make the material engaging for them. There are numerous articles and books on how to make mathematics exciting, and it would do a mathematics teacher well to read some of the works on the topic. One of the best ways I've found to make mathematics exciting and engaging is to ask students that all important question mentioned several times: "why." Why did they find the solution they did? Why does their method work? Why does a particular algorithm work? Mathematics becomes much more interesting when there is reason behind what we do. If we are given information from an outside source with little reason why we need to do what we do, then the subject becomes routine and boring, and even simply exploring why an algorithm works as it does makes the material much more interesting for students.

A common objection is that a thorough understanding of mathematics is not something many teachers possess. As Liping Ma observed in *Knowing and Teaching Elementary Mathematics: Teachers' Understanding of Fundamental Mathematics in China and the United States*, many teachers in the United States do not possess a deep understanding of the mathematics that they teach. For example, many teachers can state that one is not permitted to divide by zero, and that when one divides fractions the rule is to take the reciprocal of the second fraction and then multiply, but many teachers cannot tell *why* one cannot divide by zero or *why* one should follow the rule for dividing fractions. How do we solve this problem? Unfortunately there is no easy answer. A better college education with more deep mathematics is the best solution supplemented with good professional development in fundamental mathematical concepts. In my own mathematics pedagogy classes I often explore with my students the reasons why many of the mathematical procedures that we take for granted work. More of this kind of teacher preparation will be essential if we are to have our students gain a deeper understanding of why the mathematics works the way it does.

Students, teachers, and adults need to develop a strong number sense. Number sense is an understanding of how the number system works. Too often, people blindly follow rules and procedures without really knowing what they're doing and not really understanding how the number system works. In the following chapters it is hoped that the reader will broaden his or her knowledge of mathematical understanding gaining both better number sense and better conceptual understanding of mathematics.

The contents of this book begin with the basics structure of the number system and then progresses through basic operations, exponents, logarithms, compound interest, fractions, decimals, percentages, area of selected shapes, counting techniques, and calculus. As the book progresses, the mathematics becomes more sophisticated. The author recommends the reader attempt to understand the content of the entire book, but acknowledges that some readers may wish to stop at a certain point or ask someone for more assistance. In some cases, skipping to other sections of the book may prove useful. For example, it might make sense to skip the sections on exponents, logarithms, and compound interest in order to get to the section on fractions after the reader read about basic operations. The book is meant to be an overview of important topics, but some readers may focus on one or more sections only.

Chapter 1: The Hindu-Arabic Numeral System, Place Value, and Basic Operations

The Hindu-Arabic Numeral System and Place Value

Understanding the Hindu-Arabic numeral system is essential to fully understanding more complicated concepts in mathematics. If you either have lived in or have visited an Arabic speaking country in the Middle East you might be confused to know that the Hindu-Arabic numeral system is the system used in much of the world, yet the standard ten digits used in the Hindu-Arabic system are different than the ten digits used in many Arabian speaking countries in the Middle East today.

However, it's not the symbols that are used to represent the numbers that are so important, but rather the place value system that is used in the Hindu-Arabic numeral system. The symbols currently used in much of the world (0, 1, 2, 3, 4, 5, 6, 7, 8, 9) derived from symbols developed in India about 2300 years ago. However, the system behind the Hindu-Arabic numeral system was developed sometime between the 1500 and 2000 years ago. It is called the Hindu-Arabic system because Persian mathematicians communicated the Indian ideas to Arabic mathematicians. Arabic mathematics improved the system, and then communicated this to European mathematicians. From this perspective, it is clear to see why we named the system that we use today. This process of communication for this system to Europe began about 1000 years ago, but was not fully adopted by Europe for another several hundred years.

In order to understand the Hindu-Arabic numeral system we must first understand how place value works. Since there are only ten digits used in this system we call our system a base ten system. It is speculated that we use the base ten system because humans have ten fingers on which to count. In any n base system there are always n digits used. The symbol for the *nth* term is always a "1" and a "0" together, and in our case that number is ten. The n -1 term is always the last symbol that is used. For example, in a base seven system we would have 0, 1, 2, 3, 4, 5, 6 as symbols. The number "7" would be represented by 10.

Place value is important to consider. For example 437 is a different number than 374. In the first case, 437 means 4 hundreds, 3 tens, and 7 ones. In the second case we have 3 hundreds, 7 tens, and 4 ones. This means that the Hindu-Arabic numeral system is both additive and multiplicative. In other words, 437 can be written as 4 x 100 + 3 x 10 + 7 x 1. We can say that 4 is in the hundreds place, 3 is in the tens place, and 7 is in the ones place. We can take this one step further and write 437 as $4 \times 10^2 + 3 \times 10^2 + 7 \times 10^0$. Of course, we need to recognize that 10^0 is simply 1 since any non-zero number to the zero power is 1. We'll address more on zero to the zero power later. Zero serves us very well as a place holder when we are missing a place. For example, 302 means 3 hundreds, 0 tens, and 2 ones. Without zero, we would have no way of distinguishing a number such as 302 from 32, for example. Zero has a rich history in mathematics and is a topic worth examining outside the scope of this book. I address this history to some extent in my book, published by Wiley in 2014, called *The Development of Mathematics Throughout the Centuries: A Brief History of Mathematics in a Cultural Context.*

The Roman numeral system is an example of a system that is only additive and not multiplicative. We add or subtract the symbols to represent numbers. For example, VI is $5 + 1$ to yield 6. IX is $10 - 1$ to yield 9. Many people only encounter Roman numerals on old buildings or at the end of films to indicate the date they were made. *The Wizard of Oz*, for example, was released in MCMXXXIX. This means $1000 + (1000 - 100) + (10 + 10 + 10) + (10 - 1)$, which yields 1939. There is a definite advantage in mathematics for using the Hindu-Arabic numeral system to the Roman numeral system. For example, try to multiply a several digit number by a several digit number using Roman numeral representation and you will likely become quickly frustrated. In the English language, and many other languages originating in Europe, we use the Roman or Latin alphabet. However, it is fortunate for us that we only use the alphabet and do not use the Roman numeral system. Instead, we have adopted a better system that was developed outside of Europe.

We can extend this analysis to decimal numbers as well. For example, if we have 437.91, we could write this as $4 \times 100 + 3 \times 10 + 7 \times 1 + 9 \times 1/10 + 1 \times 1/100$. This is because 9 is the tenths place and 1 is in the hundredths place. Similarly, we can write this as $4 \times 10^2 + 3 \times 10^2 + 7 \times 10^0 + 9 \times 10^{-1} + 7 \times 10^{-2}$. Note that 10^{-1} is 1/10 and 10^{-2} is 1/100. Decimals will be address later.

Types of Numbers

Several types of numbers we will consider in this book are the following. In the real numbers system, we start out with natural or counting numbers (i.e., 1, 2, 3,…). These are the numbers that come naturally to us when counting discrete objects in the real world. We add zero to the list to get whole numbers (i.e., 0, 1, 2, 3,…). We add signed numbers to have the integers (…-3, -2, -1, 0, 1, 2, 3,…). A rational number is the quotient of two integers (for example, a and b are integers to have a/b) in which the denominator (b in this case) cannot be zero. We will see why we can't have zero in the denominator later in this chapter. We use the term "rational" because of the ratio aspect of these numbers. Rational numbers will be addressed in the next chapter.

Addition of Whole Numbers

This background in the Hindu-Arabic numeral system helps us understand how basic operations such as addition and subtraction work. For example, 36 + 21 is 57. The procedure is we add the 6 and the 1 to yield 7, and we next add the 3 and the 2 to yield 5. However, the digits 3 and 2 do not really mean "3" and "2." Rather, because of the place value, they represent 30 and 20. Hence, when we write 57 as our answer we are really saying that the 30 + 20 part gave us 50 and since 6 + 1 is 7, so we now have 57 as our answer. Subtraction works similarly. For example, 36 − 21 is 15. Again, we may think of the tens place as 3 − 2 to get the "1" in 15. However, it is really 30 − 20 to give us 10. With 6 − 1 = 5, we now have 10 and 5 to give us 15.

The above examples were simple in that there were no cases of "carrying" for addition or "borrowing" for subtraction. As a side note, borrowing is the term in which the reader may be most familiar. However, a better accepted term is "renaming." However, personally, I find the term "shifting" to be best, but renaming is typically used today. Let's look at an example of carrying with addition. If we add 34 and 18 we first add the ones using the traditional method. We have $4 + 8 = 12$. However, we are adding ones only and we do not want to write this as follows:

$$\begin{array}{r} 34 \\ + 18 \\ \hline 12 \end{array}$$

Instead, we would prefer to keep the 2, since they are the ones, but do something else with the 10 (because

10 + 2 = 12). By carrying the "1" and writing it over the 3 we are then able to add 1 + 3 + 1. This literally means 10 (from our 18) + 30 (from our 34) + 10 ("carried" from the ten part of the 12 we had from 4 + 8). Adding 1, 3, and 1 yields 5. In other words, 10 + 30 + 10 is 50. So by writing the 5 under the 3 and the 1 in the tens column, we have an answer of 52.

$$\begin{array}{r} {}^{1}34 \\ +18 \\ \hline 52 \end{array}$$

Subtraction of Whole Numbers

For subtraction we are examining 34 − 18. Since we cannot subtract 8 from 4 using the traditional method, we can "shift" 10 units from the 30 part of 34 over to the 4 ones. Taking 10 from 30 gives us 20, and the 4 (from the 34) and 10 (shifted from the 30) gives us 14. Now we can subtract 8 from

14 to yield 6. We no longer have $30 - 10$, but rather $20 - 10$. Hence our answer is 16.

$$\begin{array}{r} 34 \\ -18 \\ \hline \end{array}$$

$$\begin{array}{r} 2^{1}4 \\ -18 \\ \hline 16 \end{array}$$

By understanding place value and how the Hindu-Arabic numeral system works, we are able to understand the traditional methods for addition and subtraction. If the reader is a parent/guardian, teacher, or someone who interacts with children, having this understanding will better help the reader convey mathematics with understanding to a child. Unfortunately, many people, perhaps including the reader and certainly including the author, grew up without this conceptual understanding. It is extremely important for students to have a solid foundation of understanding rather than simply memorizing procedures. Now that we have a grasp of addition and subtraction, let's shift our focus to multiplication.

Multiplication of Whole Numbers

As a professor of mathematics education who firmly believes in learning for conceptual understanding rather than simply focusing on procedure knowledge and memorization of rules, many might find it surprising that I believe children need to memorize their multiplication tables. In fact, I would extend this memorization to the basic facts, which is addition, subtraction, multiplication, and division of single digit numbers. Memorization of multiplication tables leads to quick recall that allows people to work through problems with more efficiency.

An emphasis should be placed on the multiplication tables from 0 to 9. It is unnecessary and undesirable to have children memorize multiplication facts above 9. The multiplication facts for 10 need to be understood along with place value, and traditionally pose little problem for many children. Learning multiplication facts for 11 and 12 are not needed since children can work these out using multi-digit multiplication. Even for the 0 to 9 multiplication tables, many do not pose a problem for many children. For example, children learn that zero times any number is zero and that 1 times any number is the number itself. For the number 2, children learn that 2 times any number yields double that number. Five usually poses little difficulty for children since all products of 5 and another number yield a number that ends in a 0 or a 5. Nine can be difficult, but it

31

does not have to be. A trick many children often employ is as follows. Let's multiply 9 by 4. First, place your hands on a table. Then, counting left to right, curl your fourth finger under your hand. On the left side of that finger you have three fingers. On the right side you have six fingers. Hence, 9 x 4 is 36. This works for other single digit multipliers of 9.

The multiplication tables that pose the most difficulty for children are the 3, 4, 6, 7, and 8 tables. However, be aware that many elements of these tables have been covered by easier tables such as 1, 2, 5, and 9. Difficult memorization is not as difficult as it may first appear.

It is true that children need to understand how multiplication works and that it is really repeated addition. For example, 3 x 4 could mean 3 groups of 4, or 4 groups of 3, depending on one's perspective.

Three groups of 4 means $4 + 4 + 4$, which yields 12.

However, for larger numbers, such as 8 x 9, it would

be too time consuming to work out 8 groups of 9. It is

much more efficient to memorize that 8 x 9 is 72.

However, memorizing these basic facts alone is not

sufficient. Understanding what multiplication means,

that is, repeated addition, is important for conceptual

understanding of mathematics.

A more visual representation of multiplication

would be using area boxes. For example, 3 x 4 could

be represented as follows. There are four boxes on the

top side and three boxes on the left side. Taken as an

area model, this yields 12 boxes.

A common lack of understanding occurs when using the traditional method of multi-digit multiplication. For example, if we have 34 x 17 we normally begin by multiplying the 4 and the 7 to yield 28. However, like in multi-digit addition, we cannot write 28 as follows.

$$\begin{array}{r} 34 \\ \times\,17 \\ \hline 28 \end{array}$$

Instead, we record the 8 under the multiplication bar and "carry" the 2.

$$\begin{array}{r} {}^{2}34 \\ \times\,17 \\ \hline 8 \end{array}$$

Next, the traditional method requires that we multiply the 7 from 17 by the 3 from the 34. The important thing to remember here is that we are not multiplying 7 and 3. Rather, we are multiplying 7 and 30 since the 3 is in the tens place. Further, the 2 that was "carried" represents not 2, but rather 20. We are essentially holding on to the 20 until we have a place to put it. Once we multiply 7 and 30 to yield 210, we now have a tens place to add the 20 we have not yet recorded.

We can now add the 20 to the 210 to yield 230. This means we now have the following.

$$
\begin{array}{r}
34 \\
\times\, 17 \\
\hline
238
\end{array}
$$

...

Next we shift our attention to the 1 in 17, which is really 10. We multiply the 1 from 17 by the 4 from 34. Since the 1 is really a 10, we get 40 and not 4. The problem with calling this a 4 leads many to believe that it's just a rule that states to insert a zero under the 8 in 238 and proceed onward. An understanding of place value allows us to understand how this rule originates. That is, the zero is from the 40 we have, even though we now will simply read it as 4. Next we multiply 1 by 3, which is really 10 by 30. This produces 300. However, we already have the tens and ones places occupied by 40, so we need only record the 3 from the 300, which is conforming to the rule. Hence, we yield the following.

$$
\begin{array}{r}
34 \\
\times 17 \\
\hline
238 \\
+340 \\
\hline
578
\end{array}
$$

We add the 238 and 340 together to yield 578 because we essentially multiplied in two parts: 34 x 7 and 34 x 10. Notice we say "10" and not "1." We have 34 x 7 is 238 and 34 x 10 is 340. We can do this because of the distributive property, which states $a(b + c) = a$ x $b + a$ x c. This property is extremely useful in mathematics and we do not need to demonstrate its validity. It is taken as a mathematical property and is inherently true. In our example, we essentially have 34(17) represented as 34(7 + 10). This enables us to compute 34 x 7 and 34 x 10 separately to yield our final result of 578.

A final note needs to be made about the "zero placeholder" rule. If we were multiply with three or four digit numbers we would continue using the rule that we must add two zeros for the third line, three zeros for the fourth line, and so on. For two zeros, since we would be multiplying by a number in the hundreds place, we can understand why we would need two zeros in the placeholder.

Division of Whole Numbers

Finally, we turn our attention to division. Division is arguably the most difficult of the four basic operations. The essential task for division is to determine how many times a number (the divisor) needs to be multiplied (the quotient or in this case the answer we seek) to reach another number (the dividend). For example, we have 2 as the divisor, 3 as the quotient, and 6 as the dividend in the following.

$$2\overline{)6}^{\,3}$$

The traditional method of doing this can be understood if we consider place value. For example, we may wish to find 84 divided by 3. Using the traditional method we could write this as follows.

$$3\overline{)84}$$

To begin we would first determine how many 3's we need to multiple by to reach 8 (which is really 80 and not 8, but we'll just consider the 8 for a moment). We determine that 6 is the closest we can get to 8, which is 3 x 2, because 9 (or 3 x 3) is too large. However, recall that when looking at this from a place value perspective we know the 8 is not really 8, but rather 80. This means we have 3 x 20, which yields 60. To represent 60 without the zero we can simply place the 6 under the 8 to hold the tens place, but I prefer to write 60 instead of 6. Now we have the following.

$$
\begin{array}{r}
2 \\
3\overline{)84} \\
60
\end{array}
$$

Next we subtract 60 from 84 to yield 24. We do this because we've already accounted for 60 of the 84 in which we started and only have 24 left in which to account. We thus have the following.

$$
\begin{array}{r}
2 \\
3\overline{)84} \\
60 \\
\overline{24}
\end{array}
$$

We now determine how many 3's are needed to multiply to reach 24. Since the answer is 8, we may place the 8 above the 4 in 84, which is in the ones place. Finally, we have the following.

```
      28
   3)‾8‾4‾
      60
      ‾‾
      24
      24
      ‾‾
       0
```

Essentially we have 3 x 20 + 3 x 8 = 60 + 24 = 84, in order to check our work. If we factor a common 3 out of the expression keeping in mind the distributive property (from 3 x 20 + 3 x 8) we have 3(20 + 8) = 3 x 28. Therefore, we need 28 3's to reach the 84.

If we have a case in which we need to find a number that is not a multiple of the divisor, we will have a remainder at the end. For example, 85 divided by 3 will have a remainder of 1. Thus, in this case we have an answer of 28 with a remainder of 1, found in a similar way in which 84 divided by 3 was found.

$$\begin{array}{r}
28 \\
3{\overline{\smash{\big)}\,85}} \\
\underline{60} \\
25 \\
\underline{24} \\
1
\end{array}$$

Often students will know that they are not supposed to divide by zero, but they don't know the reason for this prohibited computation. On a conceptual level, we can understand that the idea of dividing a number of items by nothing does not make any sense. However, we can examine this mathematically. Let's say we have $\frac{8}{4} = 2$. Another way of stating this is that 4 x 2 = 8. What if we have $\frac{8}{0}$? We can imagine that $\frac{8}{0}$ is equal to some unknown quantity x. Thus, we have $\frac{8}{0} = x$. Another way of stating this is 0 times x equals 8, or $0x = 8$.

What possible value could x be? Any value substituted for x would always yield zero, and never 8. This establishes the fact that any number divided by zero has no solution, but what about $\frac{0}{0}$? We might have $0x = 0$, and of course one value for x could be zero. However, any value for x would still make the statement true. This means that there is no unique value for x, which means that we can conclude that again there is no solution.

Operations on Integers

In this section we will explore the basic operations on the integers, or signed numbers. We will restrict ourselves to the basic operations on the integers for this discussion. First, a definition for absolute value is needed. The absolute value of a number is its distance from zero on the number line without consideration of direction. When we are concerned with direction, we can use signed numbers.

For addition and subtraction the best analogy that can be employed is money and debt. For addition of two positive numbers we simply add the numbers together to get a larger positive number. For two negative numbers we can consider being in debt and taking on more debt. For example, if we are $5 in debt, and we borrow another $2, we are now $7 in debt. This can be represented as $-5 + -2 = -7$. This helps us understand the rule that if we have the same sign we add the absolute values of the numbers and retain the sign of our two original numbers.

If we have opposite signs we can proceed as follows. For example, if we are $5 in debt, and we earn $2, this allows us to pay $2 back of our debt. Logically, this would leave us with $3 of debt. We can represent this as -5 + 2 = -3. For another example, imagine we are $5 in debt, but we earn $9. This allows us to pay back the $5 and keep an additional $4 of our earnings. This can be represented as -5 + 9 = 4. The rule is that when adding signed numbers of opposite signs we subtract their absolute values and keep the sign of the larger absolute value number. A visual example might be beneficial. We can consider the shaded region to be the debt, the light region is money we earn, and the middle color (off white or light grey) will be the cancellation of debt. If we have $5 in debt and then earn $9, we have the following to have a positive $4.

+

=

=

We can analyze signed numbers with subtraction by staying with our debt model. Imagine that we are $5 in debt and we want to remove $2 of debt. Logically this would leave us with $3 of debt. We can represent this as $-5 - (-2) = -5 + 2 = 7$. The rule is that when subtracting a negative number we change the double negative to positive. People often remember this rule using the double negative rule in the English language. For example, "I am not *not* going to the store today." This really means the speaker is in fact going to the store. Another way people remember the rule is, "Two wrongs do not make a right... but in mathematics they do!" Although these help people remember the rules, they do not explain the reason why we use the rules that we do. That is why we instead choose to *reason* how the rule works.

The multiplication of signed numbers may be more difficult to understand. We essentially have three cases in multiplication: positive times positive, negative times positive, and negative times negative. We left out the positive number times a negative number case since it's the commutative property case of a negative number times a positive number (a x b = b x a). For a positive number times a positive number there isn't much that needs to be said. This is the typical case that children learn early in their education and can be represented using physical objects. Multiplying a negative number by a positive number is more difficult to understand. Similar to the addition of signed numbers, we can again consider financial debt to be instructive of this process. If we are in debt $5, we can again represent this as -5. If we are unfortunate and double our debt, we would be $10 in debt, represented by -10. This means we have -5 x 2 = -10. Similarly, if we have tripled our debt, we would be $15 in debt. This means -5 x 3 = -15.

Multiplying a negative number by a negative number is a little more difficult to understand. Consider that we are $5 in debt again. If we remove this debt we could consider this to be -5 x -1 = 5. The 5 on the right is a gain of $5 (-1 is one "removal" of debt). We may now be completely broke, but we essentially gained money in that we had our debt removed. So if we have $5 in debt removed twice, we would have -5 x -2 = 10. This means we essentially gained $10. To help better understand this, imagine we were really in debt $100. This means that if someone removes our $10 of debt, we still owe $90. However, we are $10 wealthier than we were previously. Division is similarly demonstrated as we had with multiplication.

Another approach to signed number multiplication is to use progressions. We know that

3 x 5 = 15

2 x 5 = 10

1 x 5 = 5

0 x 5 = 0

Notice that the left side decreased by 1 throughout the progression. Notice that the right side decreased by 5 throughout the progression. Therefore, -1 x 5 should give us -5, in other words 5 lower than zero. Hence, we have -1 x 5 = -5 from the pattern. We would next have -2 x 5 = -10.

3 x 5 = 15

2 x 5 = 10

1 x 5 = 5

0 x 5 = 0

-1 x 5 = -5

-2 x 5 = -10

Since we've established this, we can start again with the following.

3 x -5 = -15

2 x -5 = -10

1 x -5 = -5

0 x -5 = 0

Notice that the left side decreased by 1 throughout the progression and the right side increased by 5. Hence we would next yield -1 x -5 = 5. We would next have -2 x -5 = 10.

3 x -5 = -15

2 x -5 = -10

1 x -5 = -5

0 x -5 = 0

-1 x -5 = 5

-2 x -5 = 10

In the next chapter we will talk about everyone's favorite topic: fractions. However, we will approach fractions from a conceptual understanding perspective and hopefully remove some of the fear many people have of fractions.

Exponents

It is often convenient to use exponents to write a mathematical expression involving the multiplication of multiple factors such as a x a x a x … x a. In this case, we would write this as a^n in which we shall restrict a to be a non-zero integer right now, and n shall be restricted to positive integers for this discussion. For example, if we have 2 x 2 x 2, we have 2^3, which equals 8.

There are particular rules for operations on exponential expressions. For example, students learn that $a^m \text{x } a^n = a^{m+n}$ and that $(a^m)^n = a^{mn}$. These two identities can be easily mixed up, but this confusion does not have to be the case. Let's first look at an example. We can reason out why $a^m \text{x } a^n = a^{m+n}$. If we take the following example, $a^3 \text{x } a^2$, we can realize this means $(a \text{ x } a \text{ x } a) \text{ x } (a \text{ x } a)$. Simply counting the a's gives us $a \text{ x } a \text{ x } a \text{ x } a \text{ x } a$, which is a^5. Now, let's examine $(a^m)^n = a^{mn}$ by looking at an example, $(a^3)^2$. We can write this as

$(a \text{ } x \text{ } a \text{ } x \text{ } a)^2 = (a \text{ } x \text{ } a \text{ } x \text{ } a) \text{ } x \text{ } (a \text{ } x \text{ } a \text{ } x \text{ } a)$. Simply

counting the a's gives us a^6. By looking at simple examples of each case, one is much less likely to confuse the two identities.

Similarly, we can consider $a^m / a^n = a^{m-n}$. If we take the following example, $a^5 x \ a^2$, we can realize this means $(a \times a \times a \times a \times a)/(a \times a)$. Simply canceling the 2 a's in the numerator with the 2 a's in the denominator gives us a^3.

Earlier it was mentioned that we have an issue with zero to the zero power. Why is that? Well, it has to do with requiring a unique answer for zero to the zero power. Let's look at it this way. If we have any positive integer to the zero power, let's call the number a, we have $a^0 = 1$. However, zero to any positive integer is always zero. For example, 0^3 is 0 x 0 x 0, which is zero. Thus, we run into a problem here because we have zero to any positive integer is zero, while any positive integer to the zero power is 1. So what is zero to the zero power? Is it zero or one?

Mathematicians often define zero to the zero power as 1 for convenience. However, I prefer to leave it undefined as many others do.

Many may not realize that square roots, and any root for that matter, are exponents of sorts. For example, the square root of a number n is $n^{\frac{1}{2}}$, which is n to the 1/2 power. For cube root, we would have $n^{\frac{1}{3}}$, and so on. While it is quite straight forward in taking the square root of perfect square, such as 1, 2, 4, 9, 16, 25 (or 1^2, 2^2, 3^2, 4^2 and 5^2, respectively), it's much more difficult for non-perfect squares. One method I explained in my mathematics history book is from the Babylonians. The Babylonians found square roots by a method of averaging. For example, for the square root of 10 one might guess 2, but 2 is too low. Next, we divide 10 by 2 and have 5. Thus,

the answer is between 2 and 5. We find the average is
$(2 + 5)/2 = 3.5$. So let's divide 10 by 3.5 and we yield
about 2.9. We take the average again with the
previous estimate and yield $(3.5 + 2.9)/2 = 3.2$. We
can keep repeating this process as we get closer to
approximately 3.162, a good approximation for the
square root of 10. The square root of 10 is an
irrational number, just as is the number pi. An
irrational number cannot be represented as the ratio of
two integers. Its decimal expansion is non-
terminating and non-repeating. While we are on the
topic of pi, let's take a brief look at this interesting
irrational number.

Pi

It is possible that while many have been
exposed to pi and formulas surrounding it, many may
still not know what it really means. In my

mathematics history book I explain that pi is the ratio of the circumference to the diameter of a circle. In other words, if we measure a circle to be one meter across (the diameter), then if we wrap a measuring tape around the circle we would have approximately 3.14159 meters. This mental picture may help people understand what we mean by pi, which is very useful in mathematics but likely not often understood by many. Understanding the concept of pi can help us understand the formula for the circumference of a circle to be $C = 2\pi r$, where C is the circumference of the circle and r is the radius of the circle. Since the radius is half of the diameter, or the width across the circle going through the center of the circle, we see that for radius of 1/2 (which is a diameter of 1) we have simply pi units in circumference. In other works, $C = 2\pi(1/2) = \pi$. It would be helpful here to define what we mean by a circle, even though most people would know what I mean when I say "circle." A circle is a case in which we can consider to have a set of points equidistant from a given point, which is the center. This distance is the radius, as already discussed.

In my mathematics history book I discuss Pi Day, which was founded by Larry Shaw in 1989. Pi Day takes place on March 14, the day before the Ides of March, which was the death of Julius Caesar in 44 BCE. However, Pi Day has nothing to do with Caesar. Instead, March 14 is important because it can be written as 3/14, which indicates the approximation of pi as 3.14. Pi minute is 1:59 am or pm, with pm preferred for the school day, since a better approximation of pi is 3.14159. We can even go as far as pi seconds as 1:59 and 26 seconds could represent pi's approximation of 3.14159265358979. Pi Approximation Day is July 22, a day not included in the standard school year, because 22/7 is a popular approximation of pi. In 2009 the United States Congress official recognized Pi Day as National Pi Day. Pi Day is celebrated in some schools with eating of actual pie and discussing mathematics. On March 15, 2015 we had a unique occurrence. We essentially had 3/14/15 with an interesting time of 9:26 am or pm. We could even add 53 seconds to this if we like.

There have been people who have memorized pi to tens of thousands of decimal places. I currently have pi memorized to 225 places. Why did I do it? Is there any usefulness to knowing pi to many places? Sadly, there is none. I memorized pi to many places simply to entertain my students and show off every now and then. There is no genuine mathematics

utility in knowing pi to that many places.

Logarithms

In its most basic form a logarithm is

essentially another way of expressing an exponent. If

we have $b^x = N$, then we can express this as

$\log_b N = x$. For our discussion here let's keep b,

which is read as the base, to be a positive integer not

equal to one and keep x to be a positive integer. We

could have other numbers for b and x, but for

simplicity we will restrict ourselves for this

discussion. I would like to call x the exponent and N

the number. It helps for you to take your finger and

place it on the b in the second expression:

$\log_b N = x$. Next, move your finger to the x and then

to the N. Say to yourself, "b to x equals N." My

students have found that this kinesthetic motion helps

them remember this definition. We read this as "log base b of N equals x."

I also give background on the history of the logarithm in my mathematics history book. Scottish mathematician John Napier, who was born in 1550 in Edinburgh discovered the logarithm, which as we saw is the inverse of the exponential function. It is highly useful in efficient computing in a time before calculators and computers. Logarithms are still useful in measuring earthquakes and the logarithmic spiral appears in nature, such as in the nautilus shell. Napier published a book that contained logarithmic tables in 1614 called *Description of the Wonderful Canon of Logarithms*.

An example of a logarithm is $\log_2 8 = 3$ as we can see that $2^3 = 8$. If we have log base 10, we simply omit the base. For example, we can express

$\log 100 = 2$ as we see that $10^2 = 100$. If we have log

base e, for the exponential number e, we write this as

the natural log, or ln. For example could have,

$\ln 2.718 = 1$ as we see that $e^1 = 2.718$. The reason we

write the "l" before "n" is this is likely due to Latin or

French, in which we would have "log naturalis" or

"logarithme naturel," respectively. Note that 2.718 is

an estimate for e, which like pi is an irrational

number.

The constant e can be defined as the limit, as n

goes to infinity (or gets very large) of $\left(1 + \dfrac{1}{n}\right)^n$. If we

take values for n, such as 10, 100, and 1000, we see

we have 2.594, 2.705, and 2.717, respectively. Notice

as n gets larger, we get closer to 2.718.

There are rules in which we can develop

involving logarithms that helped us calculate without

electronic calculators in the past. One such rule states $\log_b(xy) = \log_b x + \log_b y$. We can let

$\log_b x = M$ and $\log_b y = N$. This means we have

$b^M = x$ and $b^N = y$. This means if we multiple the

left sides we have $(b^M)(b^N) = xy$. Using a rule of

exponents we know that $(b^M)(b^N) = b^{M+N}$. Thus, we

have $b^{M+N} = xy$. Now, let's think about how we

defined logarithms earlier. Looking at what we have

in logarithm form we have $\log_b(xy) = M + N$.

Substituting for M and N as we initial defined M and

N, we have $\log_b(xy) = \log_b x + \log_b y$. An example

of this is $\log_2(8) = \log_2 4 + \log_2 2 = 2 + 1 = 3$.

We can similarity do this for the rule that

states $\log_b(x/y) = \log_b x - \log_b y$. Again, we have

$\log_b x = M$ and $\log_b y = N$. And again, this means

we have $b^M = x$ and $b^N = y$. If we divide the left

sides we have $(b^M)/(b^N) = x/y$. Using a rule of

exponents we know that $(b^M)/(b^N) = b^{M-N}$. Thus,

we have $b^{M-N} = x/y$. Now, let's again think about

how we defined logarithms earlier. Looking at what

we have in logarithm form we have

$\log_b(x/y) = M - N$. Substituting for M and N as we

initial defined M and N, we have

$\log_b(x/y) = \log_b x - \log_b y$. An example of this is

$\log_2(8) = \log_2 32 - \log_2 4 = 5 - 2 = 3$.

We can develop another rule for exponents

and logarithms. We have a rule that states

$\log_b x^a = a\log_b x$. In other words, the a as an

exponent can be dropped down in front of the

logarithm and multiply the rest. We can understand

this by thinking about this situation as

$\log_b x^a = \log_b (x \cdot x \cdot ...x)$ with the x's are written out a times. Using the rule from earlier, we know that $\log_b (x \cdot x \cdot ...x) = \log_b x + \log_b x + ... + \log_b x$, written out a times. Hence, we have a times $\log_b x$. Finally, that gives us $\log_b x^a = a \log_b x$. For example, $\log_2 25 = 2\log_2 5$ because we have $\log_2 (5 \cdot 5) = \log_2 5 + \log_2 5 = 2\log_2 5$.

There is an interesting logarithm identity we can consider here. We have the question of $\log_b b^x$ means. We have b to some power is equal to b^x. That power must be x! Thus, $\log_b b^x = x$. The reader can use the kinesthetic method from earlier to verify this.

Another similar interesting identity can be considered. We have the question of what

$b^{\log_b x}$ means. Let's make $b^{\log_b x} = N$. Since we have

a base b and an exponent $\log_b x$ we can say that

$\log_b N = \log_b x$. Observing this equality tells us that

N is equal to x. Hence, we have $b^{\log_b x} = x$.

Compound Interest

A typical formula used to calculate compound

interest, that is, interest that first is computed, adds to

the original amount, and then calculates again and

again for a specified time, can be expressed as

$A = P\left(1 + \dfrac{r}{n}\right)^{nt}$, where A is the new amount, P is the

original amount or principle, r is the rate, n is the

compound period, and t is the time. The compound

period is how frequently we calculate interest and add

to the principle. For example, if we compound yearly,

we may designate n as 1. If compounding monthly,

we can use 12. For weekly and daily we could have 52 and 365, respectively. For example, if we have $10,000 to invest at 5% compounded monthly for a year, we would have in one year, provided we did

nothing else, $A = 10{,}000\left(1 + \dfrac{0.05}{12}\right)^{12(1)} = \$10{,}511.62$.

Our new amount in one year would be $10,511.62. The more frequently we compound, the more money we generate. For example, if we compound daily, we have $10,512.67. Not much different, but in large quantities over large periods of time, it will make a difference.

This formula comes from the manner in which we calculate simple interest, which can be expressed by $A = Pr$ For example, $10,000 with 5% interest yields $500 because 10,000(.05) is 500. If we add this amount to the principle we have $10,500. Basically, we now have the case of $P + Pr$, or factored $P(1 + r)$. If we took another 5% interest on this new amount, we would be calculating $P(1 + r)r$. Remember, this is the interest we have. Add this to the principle after the first interest calculation and we have $P(1 + r) + P(1 + r)r$. Factor out $P(1 + r)$ to yield $P(1 + r)(1 + r)$ or $P(1 + r)^2$. We see that this was the second calculation and we see the quantity is squared. The pattern in this case is $P(1 + r)^t$, where t is the number of calculations, which can be taken as years, for instance. If an annual interest rate is calculated monthly, for example, we would only use 1/12 of the interest rate in our calculations, but be doing this 12 times in the year. Hence, we have $A = P\left(1 + \dfrac{r}{n}\right)^{nt}$.

What if we could compound every hour, or every minute, or every second... or even less than a second? We could say this approaches continuous

compounding. In this case, we may adjust our

formula, since we cannot calculate with an infinite n

as we have it stated here. We can let $x = \dfrac{n}{r}$, which

gives us $A = P\left(1 + \dfrac{1}{x}\right)^{xrt}$. We replaced xr for n in

the exponent because if we solve for n we have $n =$

xr. Next we have, $A = P\left[\left(1 + \dfrac{1}{x}\right)^{x}\right]^{rt}$. If n gets very

large, x does as well because they are directly

proportional to each other. This means the part inside

of the brackets goes to the mathematical constant e

that we explored earlier as x gets very large. We are

left with $A = Pe^{rt}$, which may look familiar to the

reader. If we compound continuously, we would have

$A = 10{,}000e^{0.05(1)}$, which is \$10,512.71.

Chapter 2: Fractions, Decimals, and Percentages

Fractions

Fractions, and operations on fractions, can be quite difficult for many to understand. Fractions pose a major challenge for younger children in their mathematical learning, as well as a challenge to many well-educated adults. In college I tutored students in mathematics and I had noticed that fractions posed a problem for high and low achieving students alike. In one case I was tutoring a student in integral calculus who told me he was that he was not able to understand the definite integral. I reviewed all of his work and noticed that he did everything correctly until the end of the problem at the bottom of the page where he incorrectly subtracted two fractions. The student understood the calculus, but he needed to review fraction subtraction.

The study of fractions is important because it creates a foundation for the study of decimals and percentages, and a solid understanding of fractions is essential for understanding later material. Much time in elementary school is dedicated to the study of fractions. Unfortunately, much of the time dedicated to fractions examines procedural operations to the neglect of conceptual understanding. Considering that modern calculators can now handle complex fraction calculations, it may be argued that understanding fraction operations is no longer very important. However, I would reply that understanding fraction operations is important to gain number sense, something essential in mathematics. Number sense is an overall understanding of numbers and their operations, and is important in understanding higher level mathematics and functioning as a mathematically literate citizen in day-to-day life. In this chapter we will examine fractions to get a deeper understanding of what they represent and the operations used with them.

The word fraction comes from Latin for "to break." Generally, a fraction is a number that represents a part of a whole. In the context of natural or counting numbers, whole numbers, and integers, fractions are introduced when we begin to speak of rational numbers. The top number of a fraction is called the numerator and the bottom number is called the denominator. For example, in the fraction $\frac{1}{4}$, the 1 is the numerator and the 4 is the denominator. An easy way to remember the vocabulary is that numerator has an "n" for "north," and denominator has a "d" for "down."

At the most basic level we can think of fractions as part of a whole. For example, $\frac{1}{4}$ can be represented visually as follows.

A visual representation helps us understanding basic operations done with fractions. For example, equivalent fractions have the same values. We can represent $\frac{1}{4}$ as $\frac{2}{8}$ or $\frac{3}{12}$. A visual representation of $\frac{2}{8}$ is provided below. Notice that the same amount of area is shaded as in the visual representation of $\frac{1}{4}$.

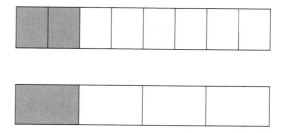

We can find equivalent fractions by multiplying the numerator and denominator by the same non-zero integer. For example, $\dfrac{1 \times 2}{4 \times 2} = \dfrac{2}{8}$.

This is true because $\dfrac{1 \times 2}{4 \times 2} = \dfrac{1}{4} \times \dfrac{2}{2}$. Since $\dfrac{2}{2}$ is equal to 1, we are essentially multiplying our original fraction by 1. Similarly, $\dfrac{2}{8} = \dfrac{2 \div 2}{8 \div 2} = \dfrac{1}{4}$. The second case would traditionally be referred to as "reducing" the fraction. This can be deceptive since the fraction maintains the same value and has not been reduced in any way. A better way of saying this would be to "simplify" the fraction into lowest terms.

Adding and Subtracting Fractions

Adding and subtracting fractions often poses difficulty for many people, children and adults alike. This is especially true when considering fractions that have different, or unlike, denominators. A visual example would help understand the operation. We'll focus on addition since fraction subtraction is essentially the same concept. If we want to find

$\frac{1}{5} + \frac{2}{5}$ we can first represent this situation as follows.

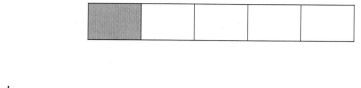

$+$

From the picture it is easier to see what we are being asked to find. Visually, we can see that the result should be as follows.

Thus, $\dfrac{1}{5} + \dfrac{2}{5} = \dfrac{3}{5}$.

If we have unlike denominators, such as

$\dfrac{1}{4} + \dfrac{1}{8}$ we can represent our situation as follows.

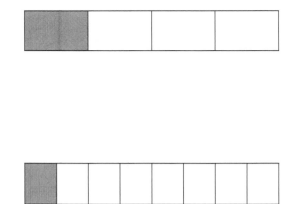

Since the shaded regions are not of equal size, it does

not make sense to add them together. This is the

reason we need like denominators in fraction addition

and subtraction. However, we can be sure to deal with

the same size pieces by breaking $\dfrac{1}{4}$ down into an

equivalent fraction. Since the denominator for $\dfrac{1}{8}$ is 8,

we can make $\dfrac{1}{4}$ equal to $\dfrac{2}{8}$ by multiplying both the numerator and denominator by 2. We can represent this as follows.

=

This means we now have $\frac{2}{8} + \frac{1}{8}$, which can be represented as follows.

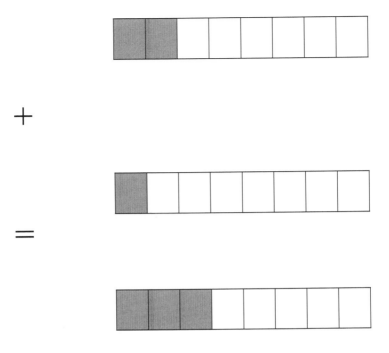

This means our answer is $\frac{3}{8}$. We can generate a

procedure that when we add fractions we first must

have like denominators and then proceed to add the

numerators together. The procedure for subtraction is

very similar.

Multiplying and Dividing Fractions

Multiplying and dividing fractions procedurally can be easier than adding and subtracting fractions. However, the procedures are often forgotten by many adults who have not used their skills in a long time. Understanding why the procedure works will facilitate better retention of the material. Similar to what we did with addition of fractions, we will examine the multiplication of fractions through a visual approach. If we want to perform the operation $\frac{1}{2} \times \frac{1}{3}$ we could represent this as follows.

X

Perhaps a better way to represent the multiplication is

the combine the two representations into a single

picture.

On the top we see that going across we have $\frac{1}{2}$ and

going down the side we have $\frac{1}{3}$. This yields the

correct answer of $\frac{1}{6}$. We can generate a procedure

that when we multiply fractions we simply multiply

the numerators together and we also multiply the

denominators together.

In order to perform the division operation on

fractions we should consider the classic adage

instilled upon students by well-meaning teachers:

"Yours is not to reason why but to flip and multiply."

This unfortunate statement is an adaptation from the

Alfred Tennyson poem "The Charge of the Light

Brigade" in which Tennyson said, "Theirs not to

reason why, theirs but to do and die." It is not lost on

us that the original imagery is one of death.

Let's consider the division of two fractions,

for example: $\dfrac{2}{5} \div \dfrac{3}{7}$. The rule is that we take the

reciprocal of the second fraction and multiply to yield

$\dfrac{2}{5} \times \dfrac{7}{3}$ to yield $\dfrac{14}{15}$. Why is this true? If we write our

problem differently, we have $\dfrac{\dfrac{2}{5}}{\dfrac{3}{7}}$. We can multiply

both the numerator and denominator of this complex

fraction by $\dfrac{7}{3}$, which is permitted since essentially we

have $\dfrac{\dfrac{2}{5}}{\dfrac{3}{7}} \times \dfrac{1}{1}$. Thus we yield, $\dfrac{\dfrac{2}{5} \times \dfrac{7}{3}}{\dfrac{3}{7} \times \dfrac{7}{3}}$. In the

denominator we have $\dfrac{21}{21}$ or 1. In the numerator we

have the rule that students are often encouraged to

memorize. We can show this abstractly using a, b, c,

and d to represent real numbers with b, c, and d not

equal to zero to yield $\dfrac{a}{b} \div \dfrac{c}{d}$ or $\dfrac{\frac{a}{b}}{\frac{c}{d}}$. We then have

$\dfrac{\frac{a}{b} \times \frac{d}{c}}{\frac{c}{d} \times \frac{d}{c}}$ or $\dfrac{\frac{a}{b} \times \frac{c}{d}}{1}$, which yields our rule.

Understanding how the rule derives will help us to

recall what we are actually doing when we divide

fractions.

Improper and Mixed Numbers

A fraction that has its numerator larger than or

equal to its denominator is considered to be an

improper fraction. For example, the following

fractions are improper: $\dfrac{5}{3}, \dfrac{7}{7}$, and $\dfrac{20}{19}$.

Conceptually, it is easier to understand improper

fractions as mixed numbers. Mixed numbers are

numbers that have an integer component along with a proper fraction component. For example, $\frac{5}{3}$ can be rewritten as $1\frac{2}{3}$. This is best explained through a visual representation.

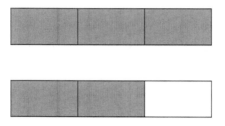

From one perspective we can see the situation as 5 parts for 3 wholes. Notice that we have gone over an entire whole. However, as a mixed number we see we have 1 full unit with an additional $\frac{2}{3}$. The visual representation should assist us in converting between improper fractions and mixed numbers. To convert from improper fraction to mixed number we see that

we must first divide 5 by 3. This will tell us how

many whole parts we have. We see that we only have

1 whole part with a remainder of 2. This yields $1\frac{2}{3}$.

Alternatively, we can consider

$\frac{5}{3} = \frac{3+2}{3} = \frac{3}{3} + \frac{2}{3} = 1 + \frac{2}{3} = 1\frac{1}{3}$. Thus, the rule we

use is divide the numerator by the denominator to get

the integer part of the mixed number. The remainder

will be the new numerator and the original

denominator remains the same. Now would be a good

time to consider what $1\frac{2}{3}$ means. It is read, "one and

two-thirds." The "and" represents addition. So we

can consider $1\frac{2}{3}$ to be $1 + \frac{2}{3}$.

To convert from mixed numbers to improper fractions we must consider the last several lines of the preceding paragraph. For example, since $1\frac{2}{3} = 1 +$

$\frac{2}{3} = \frac{1}{1} + \frac{2}{3}$, we can consider a common denominator

for 1 and 3. This give us $\frac{3}{3} + \frac{2}{3} = \frac{3+2}{3} = \frac{5}{3}$. From

this we can generate a rule that says we need to multiple the integer part by the denominator in the fraction part. We then add the numerator to this number to get our new numerator, as can be seen in the process found above. We place this final result over the denominator. We always multiply the integer part by the denominator because the denominator of the integer part is always 1. Thus, the common denominator the integer and fraction part share in a mixed number is always the denominator of the fraction part. We add the numerator at the end because we essentially have two fractions to add together with now common denominator.

Decimals and Percentages

The foundation for fractions, decimals, and percentages is fractions. We began with fractions since it sets up the conceptual foundation for decimals and percentages. Decimal comes from the Latin for "one tenth." This is essentially the treatment of fractions in which the denominator is some power of ten (i.e., 10, 100, 1000, etc.). Given that we work in a base ten system, it is convenient to represent fractions with a denominator of a power of 10. For example, 0.1 represents 1/10, 0.01 represents 1/100, 0.001 represents 1/1000, and so on. A number such as 0.13 represents 1/10 + 3/100. If we use a common denominator of 100, we then have 10/100 + 3/100 to yield 13/100. Hence we have 13 hundredths of some amount, or 13 out of 100.

In order to convert fractions to decimals we have two methods. One is the case in which the denominator is a factor of a power of 10. For example, 1/25 would not be difficult to convert to a decimal because 25 is a factor of 100. Thus we have,

$$\frac{1 \times 4}{25 \times 4} = \frac{4}{100}$$ or 0.04. We have 4 out of 100.

However, if we have a case in which the denominator is not a factor of a power of 10, we will have to divide the fraction as follows. For example, let's say we have 1/8. Since 8 is not a factor of 100, we will have to divide. We could have

$$8\overline{)1.00}^{\,0.125}$$

We found this by the following.

```
        0.125
    8)1.00
        8
       20
       16
       40
       40
        0
```

Notice that we line up the decimals for the purpose of

place value just as we did with the division examples

earlier.

Now might be a good time to talk about

decimal division. We just saw an example in which

the dividend contained a decimal point, and thus did

the quotient. What if we have a decimal divisor? For

example, consider $0.3)\overline{0.24}$. The easiest way in

which to clear this problem is to multiply the divisor

by 10 in order to have 3 instead of 0.3. However, if

we do this, we need to multiply the dividend by 10 to

yield 2.4. Why do we do this? The reason is that

$0.3\overline{)0.24}$ can be represented as $\dfrac{0.24}{0.3}$. We can then

multiply both numerator and denominator by 10 to

have $\dfrac{0.24}{0.3}$ x $\dfrac{10}{10} = \dfrac{2.4}{3}$, which is 0.8 as we keep our

place value in the quotient.

Percentage also derives from the Latin for "by

the hundred." This means if we have, for example,

13%, we are saying we have 13 parts of 100. This can

be represented as the fraction 13/100 or decimal 0.13.

Notice the percent sign indicates a fraction bar. In

order to go from a decimal to a percentage notice that

we simply move the decimal point two places to the

right and add on the percent sign. For example, notice

that 0.13 becomes 13%. In order to go from a faction

to a percentage, it may be easier to first go from

fraction to decimal, and then quickly on to

percentage. For example, 1/4 is 0.25, which can then be written as 25%. So how do students remember how to convert a percentage such as 0.0035% to a decimal? Think about simple cases such as 25% = 0.25. To go from percentage to decimal we simply move the decimal two places to the left. Hence, 0.0035% will be 0.000035, which is precisely 0.0035 per one hundred. On a quick grammatical note, "percent" is used with a given quantity, such as 13% or 13 percent. However, if we are speaking of a portion without a number, we use "percentage." For example, a high percentage of people want to know more about fractions, decimals, and percentages!

Chapter 3: Area of Selected Shapes

In this chapter we will focus on deriving the formulas for selected basic shapes. We begin with our building block for area, which can be found in a square. Each side in a square is of equal length, which means the area of a square can be taken to be side, or *s*, squared. See the figure below.

We can make a similar conclusion about the rectangle, which has an area of length multiplied by width, similar to side squared for the square. This can be symbolized as lw. See the figure below.

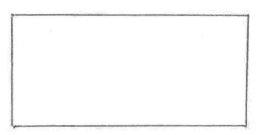

We can examine the area of a parallelogram by turning a parallelogram into a rectangle. See the figures below.

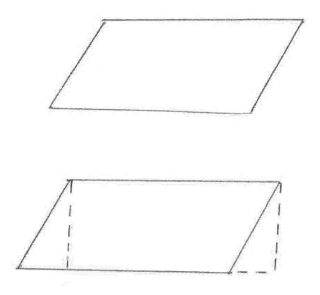

We can call the bottom of the parallelogram the base, or b, and the height from bottom to top, the height, or h. Thus, the area of the parallelogram is bh.

By cutting a rectangle or parallelogram into two triangles on the diagonal, we can create two triangles. Since the length and width of a rectangle is analogous to the base and height of a parallelogram, we can see that since cutting along the diagonal gives us two triangles, the area of the triangle is one-half the base multiplied by the height, or (1/2)*bh*. See the figures below.

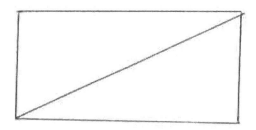

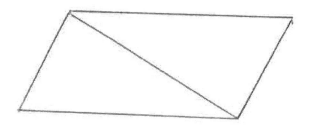

Establishing the area of the circle requires a different approach. In order to do so, let's look at an ordinary circle with radius, r. Recall the radius of a

circle is the distance between the center of the circle

and a one of the many collection of points equidistant

from the center.

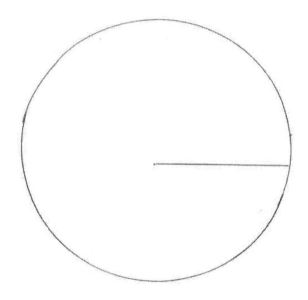

Now, we must imagine that this circle is a pizza and

that we invited many of our friends over for a party.

We only have one pizza, so we need to be certain we

have enough slices so that everyone can have a slice.

The problem is, we are very popular and have many friends. We have so many friends that the number is approaching a very large number, or even infinity perhaps. We need to make very thin slices. Now, the goal for us is to line up these thin pieces in the following manner (for the sake of the visual, the slices I have are much wider than the very thin pieces we would have).

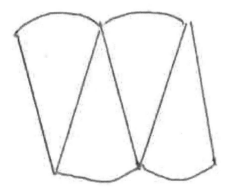

The idea here is that the slices are lined up side to side. The question we must now ask is what does the top and the bottom represented? If we think about where the slices came from the top and bottom represent the crust, or in terms of circles, the circumference. The side represents the radius. If we consider that the more slices we have, and thus the thinner the slices, the more this will approximate a rectangle. This means that the length multiplied by the width is the radius multiplied by one-half of 2π by the radius. We concluded this because we have half of the crust on top and the other half on the bottom. If the total circumference is 2π multiplied by the radius, we have half of this, hence simply pi times the radius. Hence, we should have the radius (the length of the slice) multiplied by pi multiplied by the radius. Symbolically, we have r x π x r, which gives us πr^2.

Chapter 4: Counting Techniques

Factorials

A factorial of a whole number can be represented as $n!$, which is read "n factorial." This means that we consecutively count down from n using natural or counting numbers until we reach 1. This means $n! = n \times (n-1) \times (n-2) \times \ldots \times 2 \times 1$. For example, $5! = 5 \times 4 \times 3 \times 2 \times 1$, which is 120. We have $2! = 2 \times 1$, which is 2. Finally, we have $1! = 1$ and $0!$ is also defined to be 1 by mathematicians. It is possible we may use the exclamation mark because of how shocked we should be how quickly factorials increase for relatively small values for n. For example, $13!$ is 6,227,020,800, which is quite high for a modest number such as 13.

The usefulness of factorials in mathematics can be found in applications of algebra, calculus, and probability. A useful application is found in counting techniques. For example, let's say we have 5 books to arrange. We would like to know how many different ways in which we could arrange the books. We have 5 possibilities for the first slot. Now, since one of the books is now in its place, we have 4 possibilities for the second slot, and so in. This gives us 5 x 4 x 3 x 2 x 1 possibilities, or 5!, which is 120 possibilities.

Permutations and Combinations

Another idea that utilizes factorials and is useful for counting the number of possibilities is permutations and combinations. Permutations have to do with selecting a given number from a larger or equal size group in which the order of the selections is important. The formula for permutations is

$P(n,r) = \dfrac{n!}{(n-r)!}$ where n is the size of our selection

group and we wish to choose r elements. We read

$P(n,r)$ as "n permutation r." Both n and r should be

whole numbers with $n \geq r$. Recall that when

selecting the r elements we are interested in an

ordering. For example, let's say we have a group of 5

people in which we wish to choose a president, vice-

president, and secretary. In this case we have

$P(5,3) = \dfrac{5!}{(5-3)!}$, which is

$\dfrac{5!}{(2)!} = \dfrac{5 \; x \; 4 \; x \; 3 \; x \; 2!}{2!} = 5 \; x \; 4 \; x \; 3 = 60$. This means

there are 60 possible ways to select a president, vice-

president, and secretary from a group of 5 people. We

can see how this works by designation each person as

A, B, C, D, and E. All of the three-person

possibilities, if order were not to matter, are as

follows. Notice we began with A and B, and then choose C, D, and E. We next started with A and C, and then choose D and E, and so on. There is a method behind the orderly listing.

ABC

ABD

ABE

ACD

ACE

ADE

BCD

BCE

BDE

CDE

We see there are 10 possible ways to choose three people from a group of 5 people. However, recall that we're interested in ordering the group as president, vice-president, and secretary. So let's look at one such ordering, ABC. There are 6 ways we can order ABC if the first spot is the president, second spot is the vice-president, and third spot is the secretary. Hence, we have the following. Notice the logical way we go about the ordering.

ABC

ACB

BAC

BCA

CAB

CBA

Since for the 10 possible selections we have 6 possibilities for each ordering, we have 6 x 10 = 60 ways in which to select a president, vice-president, and secretary from the 5 original people.

Another way of looking at this is there are 5 people who could fill the role of president. Once selected, there are 4 people who could fill the role of vice-president. Once selected, there are 3 people who could fill the role of secretary. Hence, we have 5 x 4 x 3 = 60 possibilities. Notice the formula for permutations accounts for this with

$$\frac{5!}{(5-3)!} = \frac{5 \ x \ 4 \ x \ 3 \ x \ 2!}{2!} = 5 \ x \ 4 \ x \ 3 = 60.$$

Earlier we discussed the number of ways we could initially select the 3 people for our positions out of the 5. We indicated there were 10 ways to do this with the orderly listing. Imagine that we were to now stop. In other words, we do not care about ordering the 3 people. We simply wish to have a committee of 3. In this case, we can see there are 10 ways to do this when we have 5 people and need to choose 3. By this we mean the order does not matter as it did with permutations. This is called combinations and the formula is $C(n,r) = \dfrac{n!}{r!(n-r)!}$. We read $C(n,r)$ as "n choose r." The reason for the division of the $r!$ component is to account for all of the repetitions of possibilities if we were to order the arrangement. For example, with a group of 5 we need 3 for a committee. When we have, for example, ABC, we could have arranged them in 6 ways because we would have 3 choices for the first spot, 2 choices for the second, and one person to take the last space. Multiplied together we have 6 possibilities. Thus, we need to divide by this amount so that we do not consider order. In this case, we divide by 3!. Thus we have $C(5,3) = \dfrac{5!}{3!(5-3)!}$, which gives us

$$\frac{5!}{3!(2)!} = \frac{5 \times 4 \times 3!}{3!2!} = \frac{5 \times 4}{2 \times 1} = 10.$$ Hence, we have 10

possibilities. Factorials, permutations, and

combinations are particularly useful in probability. A

way to remember to use permutations or

combinations is whether or not the order matters. If

the order matters, we use permutations. If the order

does not matter, we use combinations. We can recall

that a "presidential" problem means the order of

president, vice-president, and secretary matters. A

"committee" problem does not have order matter.

Permutations and president begin with the letter p,

and combinations and committee begin with the letter

c.

Chapter 5: Calculus

Calculus can be a difficult subject for many students. However, it need not be as daunting as it first appears. The two major concepts in calculus are differentiation and integration. Like learning addition and then subtraction, or multiplication and then division, differentiation and integration are two sides of the same thing. First, let's look at functions and then on to differentiation and finally integration.

Functions

A function is a relation between a domain of input values and a range of output values such that for each input there is only one unique output. The key characteristic for a function is that it affords us the benefit of predictability, something very useful to people. By that, we mean that if we know our input, we can predict the output with complete accuracy. In other words, we do not have several competing outputs that we are not sure which one will result in our particular case.

Functions are often represented by function machines. In other words, imagine in your mind a machine that take inputs and generates unique outputs. Real life examples of function machines are the old fashioned parking meters. Until recently, most municipalities had standalone parking meters, many of which took nickels, dimes, and quarters. In the city I'm from, I remember inserting a nickel and receiving three minutes of parking. A dime bought six minutes of time, and a quarter bought 15 minutes. The idea here is predictability. I knew that if I placed a dime in the slot that I would always receive six minutes of parking, no more and no less, provided the meter was "functioning" properly. That is, it was not broken. Even the new meters are still function machines, just not as visual as the old fashioned ones. Today people swipe their credit cards and indicate how much time they want. The function machine properly charges the correct amount on the credit card and gives the appropriate time on the meter.

Another example of a function machine is a vending machine. Let's say peanuts are labeled under B3 and raisins under D6. If one selections D6 the expectation is that raisins, and not peanuts, will come out of the vending machine, provided the machine is "functioning" properly.

A mathematical example of a function is $f(x)$ = $2x + 1$, where x is our input and $f(x)$ is our output. We read $f(x)$ as "f of x," that is, f is a function of x. If we take x to be 3, we can predict the function will give us 7 because $2(3) + 1 = 7$. Some functions have values for x that will not work. For example, $f(x) = 1/x$. In this case, we cannot have x equal to zero, as we saw earlier. In other cases, we have restrictions on the range of values $f(x)$ can be. For example, $f(x) = x^2$. In this case, we can see that $f(x)$ cannot take on negative values. Even if x is negative, $f(x)$ remains positive. An example of an equation that is not a function is $y^2 = x$. In this case, we can see that if x is equal to 9, we have two possibilities for y, namely -3 and 3, since both values satisfy the equation.

Derivative

The derivative measures the rate of change of a function as the input of the function changes. For example, for linear equations, such as $f(x) = 2x + 1$, the rate of change is the slope. In this case, since the function is of the form $f(x) = mx + b$, where m is the

114

slope and *b* is the *y*-intercept, we can identify the slope, or rate of change, as 2.

In my mathematics history book I explain the derivative in the following way. Since differential calculus is based upon the idea of the derivative, which is the rate of change at a given point on the curve, we could find the slope of the tangent line at the point on the curve if we want to find the derivative at that point. A tangent line is a line that passes through one point on the curve. In a curve the slope of the tangent line is changing depending on where on the curve we want to observe because the angle of the tangent line is changing as we move the point. We are looking for a way to find a function for the derivative. To find the derivative we can essentially draw a secant line, a line that passes the curve at two points, through the curve and keep making this secant line approach a tangent line. As this difference gets smaller we are approaching the derivative.

Secant Line to a Curve

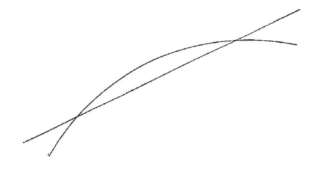

Tangent Line to a Curve

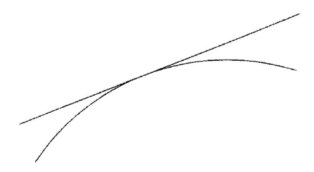

First we need to remember that the slope of a line is the rise divided by the run, which is $\frac{y_2 - y_1}{x_2 - x_1}$ or in function notation: $\frac{f(x_2) - f(x_1)}{x_2 - x_1}$. For the secant line with the points getting closer and closer, we can find the slope of the secant line, which is the idea of derivative:

$$f'(x) = \frac{f(x+h) - f(x)}{x+h-x} = \frac{f(x+h) - f(x)}{h}.$$ Since we

want the distance to be smaller and, we are essentially saying that h is approaching zero, and this is our definition of the derivative. Finding the derivative of $f(x) = x^3$ as h approaches zero we yield

$$f'(x) = \frac{(x+h)^3 - x^3}{h} = \frac{x^3 + 2x^2h + xh^2 + x^2h + 2xh^2 + h^3 - x^3}{h} = \frac{h(2x^2 + xh + x^2 + 2xh + h^2)}{h}.$$

After we cancel the h's in the numerator and denominator and let h approach zero we get

$$f'(x) = 2x^2 + xh + x^2 + 2xh + h^2 = 2x^2 + x^2 = 3x^2.$$

117

To find the derivative of a general power function, that is, $f(x) = x^n$, we can write:

$$f'(x) = \frac{(x+h)^n - (x)^n}{h}$$ as h approaches zero. We can use the binomial theorem, not explored in this handbook, to expand

$$(x+h)^n = C(n, 0)x^n h^0 + C(n, 1)x^{n-1}h^1 + C(n, 2)x^{n-2}h^2 + ... + C(n, n)x^0 h^n.$$

Since $C(n, 0) = 1$, because $(n!/(n - 0)! = 1)$ and $h^0 = 1$, we can see when we subtract x^n from the $(x + h)^n$ expansion we get the first term of the expansion cancel. With the rest of our expansion we factor out a common h to yield

$$f'(x) = \frac{h[C(n, 1)x^{n-1} + C(n, 2)x^{n-2}h + ... + C(n, n)x^0 h^{n-1}]}{h}.$$

The h in the numerator cancels with the h in the denominator, and all of the other h's approach zero. Since $C(n, 1) = (n!/(n - 1)! = n)$, we are left with

$f'(x) = nx^{n-1}$, which was developed by Gottfried Leibniz, one of the founders of calculus along with Isaac Newton, and is a very recognizable formula used in modern calculus textbooks. This makes life much easier because if we want to find the derivative of x^3 we only need to place a 3 in front, and subtract 1 from 3 in the exponent to yield $f'(x) = 3x^2$. This is much easier than using the definition of the derivative in the previous paragraph every time we need it.

Integral

Now we will consider the integral of a function. The integral is the reverse of the derivative, similar to the relationships between addition and subtraction or multiplication and division. So we can write the integral of a function x^n as follows:

$\int x^n dx = \dfrac{x^{n+1}}{n+1} + C,$ where C is a constant. We use

$\int f(x)\,dx$ for the integral with the integral "S"

symbol used because the area under a curve, found

through the integral, could be considered a

summation, or in Latin "summa," of infinitesimal

parts. Since the derivative and integral are reverse

operations we can take the derivative of our result to

see if we get back to x^n. Checking our work will

demonstrate that this works. If we integrate over a

closed boundary on the curve we shall find the area

under that curve.

   An example of the definite integral is as

follows. Let's say we want to find the area under the

curve $3x^2$ between the points $x = 1$ and 3. We first

take the integral of the function using the formula in

the previous paragraph to get $f(x) = x^3$. We can

disregard the C value when we are calculating for the

definite integral with boundary points. We thus find

$f(x)$ at $x = 1$ and 3, and subtract the two quantities. In this case we have $(3)^3 - (1)^3 = 26$. Thus, the area under the curve is 26.

Chapter 6: Unexpected Results

Mathematics is filled with many counterintuitive and unexpected results. In this chapter some examples of unexpected results will be presented that can be used in the classroom if you are a teacher, can be used at home if you are a parent, or simply just enjoyed here. Presenting students with problems that lead to unexpected results not only motivates them to study more mathematics, but also engages them in the material so that classroom management becomes much easier. Using these counterintuitive problems leads to more student interest due to the surprising nature of the results. Hopefully this leads to more interest for the reader as well.

Case 1: The Birthday Problem

This case is adapted from my article, "Motivating Students in Probability with the Birthday Problem: Presenting the Problem to Your Class and Using Technology to Support Student Learning," which appeared in *The New York State Mathematics Teachers' Journal*.

The Birthday Problem is a classic probability problem first presented by Richard von Mises in 1939. The Birthday Problem basically poses the following question: What is the probability that in a classroom with *n* number of students there is at least one birthday match (month and day, but not necessarily year)? Remember, we are not asking for a particular birthday, just any match. If we disregard leap years it can be shown that the formula for the probability of at least one match is as follows:

$P(n)_{match} = 1 - \dfrac{P(365, n)}{365^n}$, where n is the sample size

and the second P represents permutation. The formula

for $P(n)_{match}$ can also be written as

$$P(n)_{match} = 1 - \left[\left(\frac{364}{365} \right) \left(\frac{363}{365} \right) \left(\frac{362}{365} \right) ... \right]$$ with the

progression going as far as needed. The reason we

have "one minus a quantity" in both formulas is that

we are really finding the compliment of the event of

having no birthday matches. Perhaps looking at this

in the second case without permutations will help

most readers understanding. For two students the

probability of no birthday match would be $\left(\dfrac{364}{365} \right)$.

For three students the probability of having no

birthday matches would be $\left(\dfrac{364}{365} \right) \left(\dfrac{363}{365} \right)$ and so on.

For example, if we only have four students we would

have $P(n)_{match} = 1 - \left(\dfrac{364}{365} \cdot \dfrac{363}{365} \cdot \dfrac{362}{365} \right)$. Some

sample sizes and their probabilities are presented in

the table below.

Sample Sizes and Their Probabilities for the Birthday Problem

n	p
23	.507
30	.706
50	.970
60	.995

I often explore this issue with a classroom full

of students. If I have 30 students this works 70% of

the time, on average. I have students make initial

guesses first as to how many students we would need

to feel confident that we will get a birthday match.

They are often surprised by how few students we

really need. I often tell my students about the time I

was in a restaurant where there were about 50 people dining. I was telling the group at my table about the birthday problem (none of who held careers or degrees related to mathematics). One friend objected that what I was saying just simply was not true. I said that in a restaurant this size there is very likely at least one match. His reply, "I bet you $1000 dollars there is not a match in this room." Do you think I'm $1000 richer today? Well, no. I did not take the bet despite my 97% chance of being correct. Winning this money would have required me to disturb everyone's nice dinner by asking, "Excuse me, I'm sorry to disturb your lovely dinner, but I'm performing a mathematical experiment and would appreciate your participation." Also, I don't think he really would have paid anyway.

The Birthday Problem provides motivation and engagement for students to learn probability due to unexpected and counterintuitive results. An interesting historical connection can even be made by using a list of birthdays from the United States presidency. Of the 43 people to hold the office of United States president we could expect there to be at least one birthday match. James K. Polk and Warren G. Harding, the 11th and 29th presidents of the United States, respectively, both shared November 2nd as their birthdays.

Perhaps more interesting is that for the most part death days, the day on which one dies, can be seen to be somewhat as random as a birthday. Unless two people die in an accident together, we could consider the death days of the US presidents to be somewhat random. The second, third, and fourth presidents, Thomas Jefferson, John Adams, and James Monroe, respectively, all died remarkably on July 4th. In fact, Jefferson and Adams dies in the same year, 1826, unrelated to each other. Also, Milliard Fillmore and William Howard Taft both died on March 8th, 56 years apart of course.

Case 2: The Monty Hall Problem

The Monty Hall Problem is named after the host of the game show, *Let's Make a Deal*, which was on television during the 1960's and 1970's and required contestants to make a decision that was mathematical in nature. Basically, in this problem a contestant is presented with three closed doors. Behind one door is the grand prize, perhaps in this case a new car. Behind the two other doors are gag prizes, perhaps a donkey behind each. The contestant is given the option to choose a door. Let's say the contestant chooses door A. Now, if the prize is behind door A, the host of the show, Monty Hall, will open either doors B *or* C, but not both, to show you were the grand prize is not. If the prize is behind a door other than door A, then Monty will open the door where the prize is not held either from door B or C.

For instance, if the prize is behind door B, Monty must open door C to show you the donkey. If the prize is behind door C, then Monty opens door B. Now, after Monty opens a door he gives the contestant the chance to switch his or her choice. The contestant can stay with door A, or switch to the remaining closed door. The burning question of course is, what does one do in this situation?

I ask my students what they would do. Almost all (or sometimes all) say there is now a probability of 50% that it is behind door A and 50% that it is behind door C (assume Monty showed us the donkey behind door B). Very few every say there is a probability of 33% that the car being behind door A and 67% that it being behind door C. So what should one do? Well, since those are the only two plausible probabilities, I suppose one should switch since no harm (probability-wise) should come of it. It the probability is 50% for both doors, changing to door C does not matter. If the people who say it's 33% for door A and 67% for door are correct, then changing definitely has an advantage. Of course some point out that changing to door C after one selected door A, and being wrong for doing so, is psychologically painful since our contestant had the correct door at the start. Well, since this scenario appears in a chapter of a book called Unexpected Results, one could guess the latter case is the correct one. And that's true. It can be demonstrated using conditional probability and Bayes' Theorem. I won't get into the complicated mathematics here, but rather offer and easier to understand similar situation. What if there were 100 doors instead of three? Consider that our contestant first chooses door 14. Then, Monty Hall opens every door except door 37. Now the contestant must either stay with door 14, or switch to door 37. Where do you think the prize likely is? Do you think our contestant chose correctly in the beginning, or do you think there is a good reason Monty left door 37 closed?

Case 3: Law of Large Numbers Scenario

The Law of Large Numbers states that when one performs a probability experiment, such as flipping a coin, one should approach the theoretically probability associated with such an experiment after performing the experiment for a large number of trials. For example, if a coin is flipped 10 times, one might have 6 heads and 4 tails, when one might have expected 5 heads and 5 tails. This should not be surprising at all. However, when one flips a coin 1,000, or even better, 1,000,000 times, one will get closer to a 50% probability for heads and 50% probability for tails. This is where we might encounter counterintuitive results.

Let's say you play a game with one other person in which you flip a coin and get heads, you pay your friend $1. When tails comes up, your friend pays you $1. Let's say you flip the coin 10 times and get 6 heads and 4 tails. Your friend is up $6 and you're down $4 which means your friend overall has gained $2 and you have lost $2. Now, since you know that you'll approach the theoretical probability after playing enough times, you insist to keep going so that you'll get a chance to win your money back. Will this happen?

Imagine that you flip the coin 90 more times for a total of 100 flips. Let's say there are now 55 heads and 45 tails. Well, we are closer to the theoretical probability. We have 55% and 45% compared with previously having 60% and 40%. However, now you're down $10. You're closer to the theoretical probability of 50% for heads and 50% for tails. Let's say you convince the friend to play 900 more times so that we have flipped the coin 1000 times. Let's say there are now 510 heads and 490 tails. We now have heads 51% of the time and tails 49% of the time. However, you're now down $20! We're approaching the theoretical probability the more we play, however, you are continuing to lose more money overall!

We've explored several cases in probability where we find the situation to be counterintuitive. Granted probability is a branch of mathematics that more easily allows for this. However, mathematics outside of probability can have counterintuitive results as well. Take the following case for example.

Case 4: The Relationship Between $0.\overline{9}$ **and 1.**

This case is adapted from my article, "Math through Democracy? An Unexpected Result to Use in the Classroom," which appeared in the *Pennsylvania Council of Teachers of Mathematics Magazine*.

At some point during the course of my mathematics classes I ask my students to pick the correct case from the following three choices.

1. $0.\overline{9} < 1$

2. $0.\overline{9} = 1$

3. $0.\overline{9} > 1$

Students get the chance to raise their hands to vote for the correct case. I often am questioned first as to whether or not rounding is permitted. After I say that there is to be no rounding and that $0.\overline{9}$ means that the nines go on forever, the vast majority of students affirm that the first case is the correct one. Many

137

students say that the left side is only very slightly smaller than the right side, so the first case is true. The third case is immediately dismissed. However, only very few students ever choose choice number two. This happened in one of my mathematics classes when one of my students was not quite sure why he thought the second case was true, but believed so anyway. For several minutes I challenged him with statements like, "the entire class thinks case 1 is true," and "how could you think that when everyone else does not believe so." My student did not waver from his belief. At this point I decided we would investigate the situation.

I wrote on the board $0.\overline{9} = x$, where x is unknown. I asked the class what would happen if we multiplied both sides by 10. The students said the right side should become $9.\overline{9}$ and the left side should become $10x$. So now we have $9.\overline{9} = 10x$. Since we

know that $0.\overline{9} = x$, we can subtract $0.\overline{9}$ from the left

side and x from the right side to maintain our

equality. I ask students to tell me what they now have.

Students say that we have $9 = 9x$. They further divide

both sides by 9 to get $1 = x$. The conclusion is that

$0.\overline{9} = 1$. The students are simply amazed by this

result, but many are still in disbelief. They clearly

expected $0.\overline{9}$ to be less than 1. My student is

unexpectedly delighted that he was right after all.

Since many students are still in disbelief and

think that I performed some sort of "mathmagic" trick

I ask them if the following equality is true: $0.\overline{3} = \dfrac{1}{3}$.

The students affirm that the equality is indeed true. I

ask them what would happen if we multiplied both

sides of the equality by 3. The students, again

surprised, say that we get $0.\overline{9} = 1$. Most cannot

believe the simplicity of this one. Since this

demonstration is easier to understand than the

previous, more students are convinced at this point,

although, they still have trouble understanding why.

Often they find it difficult to understand the concept

that an infinite number of nines after the decimal

point would converge to 1.

For any remaining disbelievers I have the

students get out their calculators. I ask them what $\dfrac{1}{9}$

equals in decimal form. Students soon discover that

$\dfrac{1}{9} = 0.\overline{1}$. I then ask what $\dfrac{2}{9}$ equals in decimal form.

Students then see that $\dfrac{2}{9} = 0.\overline{2}$. This pattern continues

until we get to $\dfrac{8}{9} = 0.\overline{8}$ and $\dfrac{9}{9} = 0.\overline{9}$, or $1 = 0.\overline{9}$.

After establishing the fact that $0.\overline{9}$ does in fact equal 1 my class continues with a discussion about how most students believed that $0.\overline{9}$ was smaller, even if just slightly so, than 1. In addition to a discussion about the counterintuitive nature of this problem, students discuss that even though most students held an incorrect belief this does not make it true. This leads to critical thinking skills where students are better able to question commonly held, yet incorrect, beliefs. I ask further questions to more deeply explore this problem such as, "What does it mean if we cannot find any real number between two real numbers?" Students begin to explore the notion that if two real numbers have no real number in between, they are in fact the same real number.

In my calculus class I often use a more advanced approach with an infinite series. Since

$0.\overline{9}$ can be represented as $\dfrac{9}{10} + \dfrac{9}{10^2} + \dfrac{9}{10^3} + ...,$ we

can find the sum of a geometric series with $\dfrac{a}{1-r}$,

where a is the first term of the series and r is the ratio

of any term and its preceding term. Since in this case

we have $a = \dfrac{9}{10}$, and $r = \dfrac{1}{10}$, we can get the sum of

the geometric series: $\dfrac{\dfrac{9}{10}}{1-\dfrac{1}{10}} = \dfrac{\dfrac{9}{10}}{\dfrac{9}{10}} = 1.$

This activity allows students to explore the

nature of mathematics and encounter counterintuitive

results to challenge their misconceptions. Students

benefit from exploring this problem from multiple

perspectives. Students gain interest and get practice

with algebraic and numeric properties. I once had a

student who was so entrenched in the belief that

$0.\overline{9}$ had to be smaller than 1, even if slightly so, that he told me he would eventually disprove what I had presented. I thought that this was wonderful since this student prior to this was not too interested in the mathematics that we were learning. Every time I saw him in the hallway after the class ended he would tell me that he's still thinking about this and will one day prove me wrong.

It is hoped that after presenting this case students will better appreciate mathematics, learn to question commonly held beliefs, and think critically for themselves rather than simply "going along with the crowd."

Case 5: The Fibonacci Sequence

I consider the Fibonacci sequence to belong to the category of the cases here since my students are often very surprised by the ways the Fibonacci sequence appears in nature. The Fibonacci sequence, proposed by Leonardo of Pisa (called Fibonacci) in Europe but earlier recognized in India, is as follows: 0, 1, 1, 2, 3, 5, 8, 13, 21, 34, 55, 89, 144, 233, ... What is the pattern here? The pattern is that every number is the sum of the previous two consecutive numbers, given the first two initial numbers are 0 and 1. Not really that big of deal, right? Well, as said, the Fibonacci sequence appears in nature more often that one might expect. First I'll provide an example with a story. When I was an undergraduate my primary part time job was tutoring in the free tutoring center on my university's campus. Most of the tutors were undergraduate and graduate students with mathematics or mathematics related majors. Occasionally though, we would have a faculty member from the mathematics department help us with the tutoring. This person would serve as the final authority if we, the tutors, ran into trouble, or if the tutoring center became overcrowded (which it often did). One professor was a somewhat eccentric older lady from somewhere in Eastern Europe I would suspect based upon her very heavy accent. One day she brought in a pineapple with her to the tutoring room. She approached me and asked me to find the Fibonacci sequence in the pineapple. Unfortunately, I could not. She quickly exclaimed, "Then there will be no pineapple for you!" The professor then approached the next tutor with the same question and same admonition. I do not recall if anyone found the pattern and won the pineapple, but needless to say, the sequence is indeed in the pineapple.

In addition to finding the Fibonacci sequence in the pineapple, it can also be found in sunflowers, pinecones, artichokes, and nautilus shells. More interesting, perhaps, is the following hypothetical problem proposed by Fibonacci in 1202. Imagine there are two rabbits who were just born, one male and one female. Rabbits can mate after one month and the pregnancy lasts another month (meaning a rabbit can produce offspring only two months after she was born). Assume our rabbits mate after the first month and produce two rabbits that will also be male and female after another month. Our original two rabbits will keep producing two babies (one male and one female) every month forever. After one month the first set of babies are old enough to breed as well in the same manner. So after the fourth month the first set of babies will have babies (two to be exact, one male and one female). How many pairs of rabbits will there be after one year from the start of this? What is the pattern? The answer is there are 144 pairs of rabbits after 12 months. The pattern is in the Fibonacci sequence of course. When we start there is only 1 pair. In the second month there is still only 1 pair since these rabbits are pregnant. In the third month there are 2 pairs, the parents and two babies. In the third month there are 3 pairs, the parents, their older two babies, and their younger two babies. In the fourth month there are 5 pairs, the original parents, their older and younger babies, plus two new babies for the original parents, and now the oldest babies have two babies of their own. The pattern continues and we see Fibonacci models this scenario.

Case 6: How Much Money in Seconds?

The United States has been in debt nearly ever since the nation was founded. Money was borrowed to pay for the costs of the American Revolution. It stayed in the millions of dollars and researching zero briefly in the early to mid-19th Century. During World War I the US debt was in the low billions of dollars. By World War II, the US debt was almost 50 billion dollars. However, it was after the war that the debt skyrocketed into the hundreds of billions of dollars. By the Reagan administration US debt finally research 1 trillion dollars. It would reach nearly 3 trillion dollars before Ronald Reagan left office. So much for fiscal conservatism! When Bill Clinton left office US debt was over 5 trillion dollars. When George W. Bush left office, it nearly doubled to a staggering 10 trillion dollars. At the time of writing, the total debt is over 18 trillion dollars.

To be fair, perhaps looking at the US debt as a fraction of gross domestic product (GDP), or how much economic activity is generated in a country in one year, would give more information. In the years after World War II the national debt was more than 100% of GDP. This means that the money the United States government (i.e., the taxpayers) owed exceeded the amount of money generated in the United States over one year. Current United States debt is somewhat above the United States GDP of nearly 17 trillion dollars. This would put the national debt a little over 100% of GDP. Unfortunately, that percentage has been rising in recent years. Further, the United States has been taking on more debt to prevent a bigger crisis from resulting in the Wall

Street collapse in 2008. However, we should be aware that many economists promote government spending as a way to increase economic prosperity, particularly in difficult economic times to stimulate the economy. The numbers for the debt may look large, but should certainly be taken in context.

I often tell my students to imagine they were to count one dollar per second. How long would it take to count 1000 dollars? Inevitably, every time I do this someone always says 1000 seconds. Of course I want a timeframe that one could more easily understand. So how long is 1000 seconds? I often have my students make estimates as to how many hours or days it would take. It turns out that 1000 seconds is less than three hours. What about one million seconds? How long would it take a person to count one million dollars if one dollar is counted per second? Estimates for one million seconds usually vary quite a bit more. The answer is it would take over 11 and one half days, which quite a bit more time needed. What about one billion dollars? How long would it take to count using this method? Here students are surprised to find that it would take almost 32 years! This helps demonstrate the real difference between a millionaire and a billionaire. I ask the students to think privately how much they think their assets or savings accounts are worth and consider how much time it would take for them to count their money. Many see they are much closer to the person holding one million dollars than the person who has one million dollars is to the person with one billion dollars. A side discussion here could be a conversation on economic justice and inequity, certainly a worthy conversation given the magnitude of difference.

Since we are measuring one billion seconds in years it will be much easier to find out how long one trillion seconds lasts. The answer is nearly 32,000 years. Thus, 10 trillion seconds is 320,000 years. What about the national debt? If we were to pay the national debt, which is 18 trillion dollars, at one dollar per second it would take 576,000 years to pay back! I don't believe humanity will be around in 32,000 years let alone 576,000 years.

Helping students, and citizens in general, understand such a magnitude could help push spending pressure on Congress and the President so that we are able to reduce the federal deficit and start working down the federal debt, at least during good economic times when the economy is not desperate for stimulation. Again, we should consider other factors such as percentage of GDP to be useful for the conversation.

What would be the impact of sustained deficit spending past the time needed for economic recovery? The simplest answer is a reduced standard of living. Borrowing will eventually become more difficult and interest rates will invariably rise. The government will have several options. First is the unthinkable option of default, and I do not think anyone seriously proposes this option. Second is to reduce spending and/or raise taxes. Both are generally not desirable by elected officials and the public, even if necessary actions. Third is to print more money to pay the debt. This would mean more inflation and would diminish spending ability and reduce the value of peoples' savings. It would further erode the U.S.

dollar as the world's reserve currency, something from which the American people greatly benefit. There are certainly difficult challenges as many Western democracies struggle with taxation, spending, and debt, as we recently have been seeing in countries like Greece. Some economists believe we can outgrow our debt by growing the economy. However, to understand such ideas one must have a solid quantitative sense, particularly around large numbers.

Case 7: The Golden Ratio

The golden ratio was known to the ancient Greeks as one of the most aesthetically appealing ratios, and today makes its appearance in the gold rectangle, which is a rectangle with the golden proportion. The following case on the golden ration comes from my book, *The Development of Mathematics Throughout the Centuries: A Brief History of Mathematics in a Cultural Context.*

The golden ratio is the case in which we have the ratio of a large line segment to a small line segment such that the ratio is equal to the sum of the two line segment to the large line segment.

_____   _____

a b

We can take the small line segment to be a and the large line segment to be b. This means we have $b/a =$

$(a + b)/b$ or $b/a = a/b + 1$. If we let $x = b/a$, then we have $x = 1/x + 1$. Multiply x to both sides and we have $x^2 = 1 + x$, which becomes $x^2 - x - 1 = 0$. If we apply the quadratic formula, which will be addressed in a later chapter, we get $x = 1/2 + \sqrt{5}/2$ or $1/2 - \sqrt{5}/2$. If we focus only on the first root, we see that this value is approximately the irrational number 1.61803. This is the golden ratio and is named by the Greek letter phi, which is symbolized as φ. If we look at the absolute value of the negative root we have 0.61803.

The golden ratio is considered by many to be a very aesthetically pleasing ratio. It often takes the form of a golden rectangle, which is a rectangle of the proportion 1:φ. A rectangle that is close to golden would be a 3 x 5 inch index card, television screen, and the front of a cereal box. It is said that the Greek

Parthenon was built with the golden ratio in mind in the architectural structure. Some have claimed that the most pleasing human proportions in face and body have golden ratio relationships. Leonardo da Vinci called the golden ratio the divine proportion and it can be seen in his *Mona Lisa* and *Vitruvian Man*. The golden spiral, which is based on the golden ratio, appears in nature such as in the pine cone and nautilus shell.

Case 8: The Square Root of 2 is Irrational

The following text, like the previous case, also comes from my mathematics history book.

Euclid provided a nice proof to show that $\sqrt{2}$ is irrational, although it is generally agreed upon that he was not the originator of the proof. Aristotle is known to have hinted at this proof by stating that if $\sqrt{2}$ were rational all odd numbers would really be even. Euclid presented a proof by contradiction, or *reductio ad absurdum*, translated to "reduce to the absurd," which meant that we were to assume the opposite of what we were trying to prove and show that this leads to a contradiction. Hence, our original assertion must have been true. Euclid assumed that $\sqrt{2}$ was rational, which would mean $\sqrt{2} = a/b$, where a/b is a fraction in simplest form. Next, we square both sides to yield $2 = a^2/b^2$. This gives us $2b^2 = a^2$.

This means that since a^2 is even, then a must be even.

Since a is even we can write a as $2m$. Substituting this

gives us $2b^2 = (2m)^2$, which means $2b^2 = 4m^2$. This

simplifies to $b^2 = 2m$, which means that b^2 is even and

thus b is even. Since both a and b are even we have a

contradiction because this would mean the original

fraction was not in simplest form as was claimed. Our

claim is now proved and we can end the proof with

the letters *qed*, which is an abbreviation for the Latin

quad erat demonstratum, meaning it has been shown

or demonstrated.

One final point to the proof should be noted.

We assumed that if a^2 was even then a was also even.

Since a^2 is a x a, and we know that this product is

divisible by 2, then we know that one of the a's must

be divisible by two (in fact both are since they are

both the same number). This means that if a^2 is even, a must be as well.

Case 9: The Infinitude of Prime Numbers

The final case that will come from my history book involves the infinite number of prime numbers. A few years back someone told me that mathematicians found the largest prime number. I agreed that was interesting and wondered out loud if the next one would be found soon. The person insisted that the prime number found was the largest we would ever find and wondered out loud what it was exactly that I was learning in mathematics class. However, there is an important proof from Euclid that shows that there will never be a largest prime number. The following text from my history book demonstrates this.

First, recall that a prime number is a positive integer that only has two unique factors. This is usually taken to be 1 and itself. Hence, the first prime numbers are 2, 3, 5, 7, 11, 13, 17, 19, 23, 29, 31, etc. This proof, one of the greatest of antiquity like the square root of two is irrational, is conducted in a similar manner. Before we conduct the proof we first need to establish the Fundamental Theorem of Arithmetic, which states that all numbers can be written as the product of prime numbers. For example, 6 can be written as 2 x 3 and 12 can be written as 2 x 2 x 3. For a prime number such as 5, we simply write 5. To prove this notion Euclid used a *reductio ad absurdum* proof by assuming the opposite: not all numbers can be written as the product of prime numbers. Let us state the smallest such number as n. That would mean that n, a positive composite integer, which is a positive integer that is not a prime number, could be written as $n = a \times b$ where both a and b are positive integers. Now, since n

162

is the smallest number that cannot be written as a product of prime numbers, a and b must be able to be written as the product of prime numbers. It is here we find our contradiction because this means that n could be written as the product of prime numbers after all. Hence, we conclude that all numbers can be written as the product of prime numbers. Euclid continued his proof, not discussed in detail here, to show that any two representations as the product of prime numbers are in fact the same, which means that every number has a unique prime factorization.

For our proof that there is an infinite number of prime numbers we first assume the opposite, that is, that there are a finite number of prime numbers and proceed with a *reductio ad absurdum* proof. If there are a finite number of prime numbers, we can list them as follows: $p_1, p_2, p_3, \ldots, p_n$, where p_n is the largest prime number. We can multiply all of the prime numbers together to yield: $p_1 \times p_2 \times p_3 \times \ldots p_n$. This new number is clearly composite because of all the prime factors. If we add 1 to this number we yield: $p_1 \times p_2 \times p_3 \times \ldots p_n + 1$. This is where the proof becomes interesting. This new number is either a prime or composite number. If there are a finite number of prime numbers, we can expect this number to be composite. However, what factors other than 1 and itself could this number have? It clearly cannot have any of the prime numbers as factors: p_1, p_2, p_3, $\ldots$, p_n because each of these prime numbers will be a factor of $p_1 \times p_2 \times p_3 \times \ldots p_n$. Since there are no prime factors of $p_1 \times p_2 \times p_3 \times \ldots p_n + 1$, we can conclude that this number is a new prime number. The contradiction is that we had already listed all prime numbers, and yet we found a new prime number.

Hence, there are an infinite number of prime numbers.

Case 10: The Unthinkable Case

We have been living under the threat of nuclear annihilation since the mid 20th Century. Shortly after we entered the nuclear age the threat of nuclear war has been hanging over humanity's head as John F. Kennedy described it as a "Sword of Damocles." Robert Oppenheimer, father of the atomic bomb, at the first testing in New Mexico quoted the *Bhagavad Gita* by saying, "If the radiance of a thousand suns were to burst at once into the sky, that would be like the splendor of the mighty one. Now I am become Death, the destroyer of worlds." Including the Cuban Missile Crisis, there has been at least more than several known, even if brief, false alarm nuclear crises.

The advent of the Nuclear Age is very interesting for me since I was born well after the

Nuclear Age began. Many people alive today do not know what it is like to live in a world without nuclear weapons. Humanity has held this capability for an extremely small period in human history with well under a century of life under the threat of the bomb. It would seem that the longer humanity possesses such instruments of destruction, the more likely it is that we will be destroyed by them. What sort of future then do we have? Having students, and adults, more aware of the numbers involved could perhaps have some small effect on the anti-nuclear weapon movement in the right direction. But how do we return to a world before nuclear weapons? Would not it be more dangerous for large countries with nuclear weapons such as the United States, Russia, and China to abandon their weapons? Is there too much distrust to do so?? These are difficult questions, so let's now look at the nuclear numbers.

How could a mathematics teacher connect the destruction of such a bomb to mathematics? Do students realize how much more powerful our bombs are today compared to the ones that were dropped on Japan in 1945? The bomb that fell on Hiroshima called "Little Boy" was equivalent to approximately 15 kilotons of TNT. The bomb that fell on Nagasaki called "Fat Man" was equivalent to approximately 20 kilotons of TNT. A kiloton is 1000 metric tons. A metric ton is 1000 kilograms or roughly over 2000 pounds. So that means one kiloton roughly equals over 2 million pounds of TNT, and further 15 kilotons is roughly over 30 million pounds of TNT. Twenty kilotons is roughly over 40 million pounds of TNT. This may seem like a lot to a child, adolescent, or even an adult (it does to me!). However, the largest detonated nuclear bomb was the Tsar Bomb made by the Soviet Union that was a 50 megaton nuclear bomb. You read that correctly. It's *mega*ton, not kiloton. That's equivalent to 50 million metric tons. Or in terms of the bombs dropped on Japan during World War II (which uses kilotons), the Tsar Bomb was a 50,000 kiloton bomb. That is over 100 billion pounds of TNT. This of course is an exception with many nuclear weapons today in the United States and Russia carry bombs ranging between 300 and 1000 kilotons (1000 kilotons is 1 megaton). These, however, remain obviously much more powerful than the early atomic bombs used against Japan. Today there are over 16,000 nuclear weapons in the world with many of them ready for war, and some in storage. During the Cold War in the 1980's there were over 60,000 nuclear weapons between the U.S. and Soviet Union.

Almost all adults accept this and live their lives every day with this knowledge. Most probably do not think about it. Yet it remains our Sword of Damocles. Carl Sagan once said that there probably are not any aliens in the universe advanced enough to visit Earth since a civilization would not become advanced enough for intergalactic travel before it was advanced enough to destroy itself. This is related to the Fermi Paradox proposed by physicist Enrico Fermi.

Going forward as more technological breakthroughs occur, many countries may gain access to advanced weaponry. Possibly more countries will obtain nuclear weapons than the current nine: United States, Russia, United Kingdom, France, China, India,

Israel, Pakistan, and North Korea. Further, during the writing of this book a constant news story is the question of whether or not Iran is seeking nuclear weapons and the possible nuclear deal. As more nations obtain advanced weapons and even nuclear weapons there appears to be more of a risk of at least a limited, if not catastrophic, nuclear war. Not long ago there was much fear that India and Pakistan could turn to nuclear war over disputed province, Kashmir. The effects of this would be felt around the world. Kennedy thought in his near future between 10 and 20 nations could have nuclear weapons before the end of his office. Fortunately, not as many nations have obtained nuclear weapons as Kennedy had predicted. However, nuclear proliferation will remain a serious issue into the 21st Century.

Chapter 7: Reducing Mathematics Anxiety, Collaborative Groups, and Literacy in Mathematics

This brief chapter has three components, all of which will only be lightly addressed: reducing mathematics anxiety, collaborate groups, and literacy in mathematics.

Reducing Mathematics Anxiety

A common problem for many students, and adults, as well, is mathematics anxiety. Mathematics anxiety can be defined as the uneasy feeling, in a mild case, to a high state of anxiety and fear, in extreme cases, when thinking about mathematics and having to perform in mathematics. Mathematics anxiety can be a significance hindrance to performing well in mathematics for young students, and can even affect adults as well. Mathematics anxiety has the potential to curtail student persistence in problem solving as well as their regard and engagement with the subject. In this very brief chapter we'll look at some ways to reduce mathematics anxiety.

Many researchers in the area believe that mathematics anxiety is a learned response from negative past experience with mathematics, particularly in school. This may come from negative experiences with parents/guardians, teachers, or other students. Mathematics anxiety can afflict anyone. High performance expectations can be one possible reason for mathematics anxiety. Another reason could be the humiliation of not being able to perform well in mathematics. Testing anxiety, related to mathematics anxiety, could be another aspect to this problem. Untimed testing time may be a partial solution to this problem along with giving students sample tests before the actual test day.

Mathematics is a subject that builds upon itself. The problem with this is if students begin to fall behind, later material is not easily grasped. This can lead to very negative feelings toward the subject and lead to anxiety. Additionally, teachers who taught mathematics procedurally, and not conceptually as promoted in this handbook, could have inadvertently led some students to develop mathematics anxiety. Memorizing the content rather than understanding it can lead to anxiety because this means the students never really understood what they were doing. As a preventative measure parents/guardians and teachers can work to make sure that students are *understanding* the mathematics before moving onward to the next topic, particularly as mathematics builds upon previously mastered material. This may be one of the best things that can be done to prevent students from developing mathematics anxiety. Additionally, having high expectations for students demonstrates one's confidence in the student's ability to do well in mathematics.

Another aspect that does not help students learn mathematics well is that young people are bombarded by the media with the idea that mathematics is very difficult and there is an expectation that many people will not perform well. This message is particularly directed at female students. Male and female students generally have similar performance levels in mathematics until about the fourth grade but then diverge. Why the fourth grade? Perhaps this is the time period students becomes more aware of societal expectations. There are limited steps we can take regarding the media's message, but we can at least work to counteract the message by showing that mathematics is fun, interesting, and can be understood with some effort. Parents/guardians and teachers who show they enjoy mathematics, and are enthusiastic about mathematics, can have a great impact on the students. Alternatively, showing a negative attitude for mathematics can have the opposite effect.

Helping students understand the utility of mathematics in life, such as in everyday life and career, can certainly help. As stated earlier, some of the highest paying and most satisfying jobs require mathematics skills and understanding. Helping young people to understand this reality could help them not to develop mathematics anxiety, or help to alleviate it. Additionally, showing how mathematics relates to students' own interests can help reduce the stress students feel about the subject.

Another approach to give young people is small successes. Helping students to persist in a problem can be very difficult. However, giving students small successes can show them that if they persist, they can solve the problem. Small successes could help alleviate or even prevent a sense of anxiety about the subject. Alleviating mathematics anxiety helps gives students the confidence and self-efficacy needed to persist in mathematical problem solving.

As an adult, one may find oneself with feelings of mathematics anxiety that developed as a child. While much of what has been discussed can help children alleviate mathematics anxiety, adults can work to alleviate their own as well. Reading a book like this one, among other such books, can help make sense of the basic mathematical concepts and go a long way in boasting one's confidence. Talking to other adults who feel similarly may help also. I'm not certain if anyone has ever gone into therapy over mathematics anxiety, but if one visits with a therapist, talking about this particular anxiety could certainly help.

Collaborative Groups

Educational research is very clear that students learn best when they learn with others. It comes as no surprise given that humans are social animals and work better together. Lev Vygotsky was a pioneer in promoting that people learn best when they learn together. This can be applied to learning mathematics. The research is clear that heterogeneous, or mixed ability, groups are better than homogeneous, or similar levels of ability groups. This means that the highly excelling mathematics students should also be mixed with the middle area students along with the students who struggle. The struggling students clearly benefit from the help from the excelling students. However, many worry that the excelling students will be held back. Actually, it is quite to the contrary. The excelling students will have to really understand the material in order to explain it. This helps refine the thinking of the excelling students as well. Aristotle was the one who said that those who know can do, while those who understand can teach. I find this preferable to the George Barnard Shaw version in which many are familiar.

Literacy in Mathematics

Not long ago I wrote a book chapter edited by my colleague, Fran Falk-Ross, called *Language-Based Approaches to Support Reading Comprehension* published by Rowman and Littlefield. My chapter was called, "Mathematics Talk: Literacy Development in a Mathematics Context." I will not repeat too much of what I wrote for the chapter, but briefly discuss the importance of literacy in mathematics.

In the chapter I discussed methods to help teachers integrate literacy into the mathematics class because of the importance of problem solving in mathematics. Problem solving will be addressed in the Conclusion. In order for students to be effective problem solvers, strong literacy skills are needed. The first step in understanding a mathematical word problem is to read it, which requires reading comprehension. In addition, in order for students to articulate their own thinking in mathematics, writing skills are necessary. One important connection between mathematics and literacy is the use of literature in mathematics. There are numerous books referenced in my book chapter that tell stories in a mathematical context. Another strategy is to keep student logs or journals about one's mathematical development. This helps sort out the concepts and also reinforces the connection between mathematics and literacy. Reflective essays can be helpful in which students reflect on their own background in mathematics, as well as the progress they had made.

Conclusion: Teaching Mathematics with Critical Thinking, Inquiry, and Problem Solving

Critical Thinking, Inquiry, and Problem Solving

Most students experience their mathematics educations by learning procedural techniques and calculation. They learn how to apply formulas and apply the skills they learn in class. The first part of this book addressed conceptual issues for selected mathematics concepts. In other words, the understanding of *why* the mathematics works was addressed. This is quite different than the traditional approach of only explaining *how* the mathematics works. The first part of this book can be used by mathematics teachers who wish for their students to have a better understanding of the concept.

Additionally, the research is clear that in mathematics education students learn best through critical thinking, inquiry, and problem solving. Critical thinking and inquiry mean that students are investigating, analyzing and synthesizing information. This is related to a major focus on the teaching of mathematics, namely problem solving. Problem solving is a process in which one attempts to solve an unfamiliar problem situation without immediate knowledge of how to go about solving the problem. This means the person must use previous knowledge and critical thinking to apply to the new situation. The key component is that the problem situation must be unfamiliar to the person solving it. If the person already knows how to solve the problem, it ceases to be a problem for that person. George Polya, in his classic book published in 1945, *How to Solve It*, outlined the four steps for problem solving: understand the problem, make a plan, carry out the plan, and look back. These steps are analogous to the scientific method but for mathematical problem solving.

Final Thoughts

While any book from this handbook's category could certainly cover more mathematics more deeply, the intention of this brief handbook was to give an overview of some of the more important and basic topics in mathematics while approaching it from a different perspective than many readers may have experienced while in school.

Secondly, ten mathematical cases were presented often with counterintuitive and unexpected results. The intention is to make mathematics more interesting through examples in which the results did not coincide with previously held notions and beliefs. It is hoped this will ignite further interest in mathematics for the reader or for anyone whom the reader is teaching mathematics.

Finally, a very brief chapter on mathematics anxiety was included in this handbook. It is my contention that mathematics anxiety frequently suppresses the persistence and motivation for many students in mathematics and teachers need to help students overcome their mathematics anxiety.

Mathematics is a fascinating subject and hopefully this brief handbook will be a start for further mathematical explorations. If approached from the right perspective, mathematics can be enjoyable and engaging, and understanding the deep mathematical ideas behind the basic concepts will motivate a person to want to learn more. This is a major shift in the way in which mathematics can be viewed. Best wishes on your continued mathematical journeys!

33967758R00103

Printed in Great Britain
by Amazon